EDITIONS

ARMENIAN
BULGARIAN
BURMESE
CHINESE
ENGLISH
ESTONIAN
FRENCH
GREEK
GUJARATI
HINDI
HUNGARIAN
IBAN/ENGLISH
ILOKANO
INDONESIAN
ITALIAN
JAPANESE
KANNADA
KISWAHILI
KOREAN
MARATHI
NEPALI
NORWEGIAN
ODIA
POLISH
PORTUGUESE
RUSSIAN
SINHALA
SPANISH
TAGALOG
TAMIL
TELUGU
THAI

UPPER ROOM

WHERE THE WORLD MEETS TO PRAY

Daniele Och
UK editor

INVITATIONAL
INTERDENOMINATIONAL
INTERNATIONAL

32 LANGUAGES
Multiple formats are available in some languages

BRF Ministries
15 The Chambers, Vineyard
Abingdon OX14 3FE
+44 (0)1865 319700 | brf.org.uk

Bible Reading Fellowship (BRF) is a charity (233280)
and company limited by guarantee (301324),
registered in England and Wales

EU Authorised Representative: Easy Access System Europe – Mustamäe tee 50, 10621
Tallinn, Estonia, **gpsr.requests@easproject.com**

ISBN 978 1 80039 486 5

Originally published in the USA by The Upper Room® **upperroom.org**

Cover photo by pexels.com/@julia-volk

Acknowledgements
Scripture quotations marked with the following abbreviations are taken from the version shown. Where no abbreviation is given, the quotation is taken from the same version as the headline reference.

NIV: The Holy Bible, New International Version (Anglicised edition) copyright © 1979, 1984, 2011 by Biblica. Used by permission of Hodder & Stoughton Publishers, an Hachette UK company. All rights reserved. 'NIV' is a registered trademark of Biblica. UK trademark number 1448790.

NRSV: The New Revised Standard Version Updated Edition. Copyright © 2021 National Council of Churches of Christ in the United States of America. Used by permission. All rights reserved worldwide.

CEB: copyright © 2011 by Common English Bible.

KJV: the Authorised Version of the Bible (The King James Bible), the rights in which are vested in the Crown, are reproduced by permission of the Crown's Patentee, Cambridge University Press.

A catalogue record for this book is available from the British Library

Printed and bound in the UK by Zenith Media NP4 0DQ

How to use *The Upper Room*

The Upper Room is ideal in helping us spend a quiet time with God each day. Each daily entry is based on a passage of scripture and is followed by a meditation and prayer. Each person who contributes a meditation seeks to relate their experience of God in a way that will help those who use *The Upper Room* every day.

Here are some guidelines to help you make best use of *The Upper Room*:

1. Read the passage of scripture. It is a good idea to read it more than once, in order to have a fuller understanding of what it is about and what you can learn from it.
2. Read the meditation. How does it relate to your own experience? Can you identify with what the writer has outlined from their own experience or understanding?
3. Pray the written prayer. Think about how you can use it to relate to people you know or situations that need your prayers today.
4. Think about the contributor who has written the meditation. Some users of *The Upper Room* include this person in their prayers for the day.
5. Meditate on the 'Thought for the day' and the 'Prayer focus', perhaps using them again as the focus for prayer or direction for action.

Why is it important to have a daily quiet time? Many people will agree that it is the best way of keeping in touch every day with the God who sustains us and who sends us out to do his will and show his love to the people we encounter each day. Meeting with God in this way reassures us of his presence with us, helps us to discern his will for us and makes us part of his worldwide family of Christian people through our prayers.

I hope that you will be encouraged as you use *The Upper Room* regularly as part of your daily devotions, and that God will richly bless you as you read his word and seek to learn more about him.

Signs and wonders

I have set my rainbow in the clouds, and it will be the sign of the covenant between me and the earth.
Genesis 9:13 (NIV)

The Bible is full of miraculous signs of God's presence: a rainbow after the earth was flooded, a burning bush that was not consumed, the protection of men in a den of lions, and a fiery furnace, water turned to wine, and walking on water. These are just a few of the wonders we encounter in scripture. To be honest, though, such signs are difficult for me to comprehend and they leave me a bit incredulous. Though my life has been marked by God's grace and love, I have not experienced signs and wonders like these. But I don't think signs of God's presence and love need to be dramatic or supernatural to make a significant difference in our lives.

In this issue of *The Upper Room*, writers describe ordinary events that took on new meaning because, through them, they felt God's presence. A tree growing from a rock, notes in a lunchbox that spark holy conversation, sports teams cheering each other on, an extra place set at the table – each of these are signs of God's presence and love in the world. When we pay attention to and receive ordinary moments of grace as reassurance of God's love and care, our lives become richer and more connected to God's ongoing work in the world. And when we allow this deeper connection to the Divine to shape our words and actions, we make God's presence a little easier for others to see as well. How will you remain alert to signs of God's presence in the coming weeks?

Lindsay Gray
Editorial director, The Upper Room

Where the world meets to pray

Odia edition

Telugu edition

Writers featured in this issue of *The Upper Room*:

- Carol Peter (India)
- Jaiprakash D. Roy (India)
- Hitesh J. Solanki (India)
- Elina Yeptho (India)
- Amira Emmanuel (Pakistan)

Gifts to the international editions of *The Upper Room* help the world meet to pray.
upperroom.org/gift

The editor writes...

'Our Father in heaven…'
Matthew 6:9 (NIV)

There's a phenomenon in the UK, apparently unique to us, called 'TV pickup'. This is a sudden spike in energy demand on the national grid during ad breaks in popular television events, as millions of homes around the country turn on their kettles. It is a less frequent occurrence now, as the advent of streaming services over the past two decades has changed our television viewing habits. Still, there are occasions like major sporting events when you know that as you watch the live broadcast, millions of others are at the same time doing likewise. It's a small reminder that you are part of a wider community.

The more observant readers among you will have noticed that the short prayer at the end of each meditation is always written using plural pronouns – *we*, *us* and *our* – rather than singular – *I*, *me* and *my*. I am not sure of the origin of or reasons for this editorial policy, but I suspect it has something to do with the fact that the Lord's prayer is recorded (in Matthew's and Luke's gospels) in the same way – '*Our* Father… give *us*… as *we* forgive…' It's a small reminder that since its origins, the Christian faith has been practised in community.

As the strapline on the cover says, *The Upper Room* is 'where the world meets to pray'. I hope you find it an encouragement that, as you use this issue in your daily devotionals, the passage you read and the prayer you pray is one that thousands of others around the UK, and millions around the world, are likewise reading and likewise praying with you.

A happy and blessed new year to you – or should I say, to us!

Daniele Och
UK editor

A relationship that lasts

Read Hosea 11:1–4

'I led them with cords of human kindness, with ties of love. To them I was like one who lifts a little child to the cheek, and I bent down to feed them.'

Hosea 11:4 (NIV)

I stood alone on the rooftop, watching the city celebrate with fireworks at the promise of the coming year. A failed relationship had left me feeling adrift and unsure of my place in the world. I couldn't shake the feeling of loneliness that enveloped me. As the clock struck midnight on New Year's Eve, I felt a mix of emotions – doubt, insecurity, but also a glimmer of hope for the year ahead.

In the midst of my solitude I am comforted by God's promise in Hosea 11:4. God's love, like cords of human kindness, reminded me of the love parents can give their children. Despite my brokenness, God embraced me as a father would his hurting child, lifting me up with tender care and providing peaceful comfort. I remembered that God has me in the palm of God's hand. While many people had let go of me, God was with me, holding my hand.

When I fully dedicated my life to Christ, this lasting relationship gave me the courage to form more meaningful ones with others. In my family now, though there are shortcomings, we believe that God is the foundation of our life together.

Prayer: *Thank you, heavenly Father, for your love and support. Reassure us that we are safe with you when we feel uncertain or alone. In Jesus' name. Amen.*

Thought for the day: Only God can wipe every tear, cure every heartbreak and bring us unspeakable joy.

Joseph Talusan (Laguna, Philippines)

To be continued

Read Philippians 1:1–11

I am confident of this, that the one who began a good work in you will continue to complete it until the day of Jesus Christ.

Philippians 1:6 (NRSV)

Growing up in the 1970s, before on-demand programming and video streaming, my family had one TV with three major channels. When the dramatic miniseries became a popular genre and a new episode aired, we would watch intently as tension built. Then suddenly the screen would go dark, and the words 'to be continued' would appear, leaving us in suspense. Having to wait a week to watch the next episode in the series was frustrating.

When it comes to our life stories, 'to be continued' could be God's tag line. We anxiously wait – often in frustration and disappointment – for our circumstances to change, for a new chapter to begin or for an old one to close. But we need not despair. God is actively involved in our lives.

Today's scripture encourages us that God will finish the good work God has started in us. God does not leave us disconnected or without purpose. At times we may feel we are in a to-be-continued phase of our lives, but in these moments, we can stay connected to God through scripture reading, prayer, wise counsel and church community.

Prayer: *Dear God, help us to trust you with the story of our lives. Amen.*

Thought for the day: I will look forward to what God has in store for me.

Stephanie Quattlebaum (Georgia, USA)

Never lost to God

Read Matthew 7:7–8

'The Son of Man came to seek out and to save the lost.'
Luke 19:10 (NRSV)

The money I had put aside for my church offering had somehow disappeared. It wasn't a huge sum, but I searched carefully everywhere inside the house and even looked outside, thinking it might have blown away through the open front door. Eventually I gave up and forgot all about it for several months.

On New Year's Day, I was cleaning the house and decided to rotate the seat cushions on the sofa. As I removed the last one, I found my missing money, still folded, resting against the inside of the sofa arm. It must have fallen out of my pocket and worked its way down into the folds of the couch as we sat on it day after day.

As I replayed in my mind what had happened, it occurred to me that I would have found the money sooner had I not stopped looking. I believe that is the kind of persistence we are called to in today's quoted scripture verse. I can also see how this idea extends to our relationship with God or, rather, God's relationship with each of us.

Although our sinful actions separate us from God and we at times turn our backs on God, we are never lost to God. Like a gentle shepherd, God persists in seeking us until we are found.

Prayer: *Thank you, God, that we are never out of your sight and always on your mind. Help us to remain in your presence in humble obedience to your will. Amen.*

Thought for the day: I am valuable to God.

Arlene Timber-Henry (St Maarten)

 PRAYER FOCUS: SOMEONE WHO HAS LOST SOMETHING VALUABLE

From fear to faith

Read Colossians 1:15–17

By him were all things created, that are in heaven, and that are in earth, visible and invisible.

Colossians 1:16 (KJV)

Shortly after our daughter was born, while my husband was holding her and offering her a bottle, the nurse noticed that our baby was struggling to breathe. Pushing my husband aside, the care team quickly surrounded our tiny baby who was in distress and admitted her to the neonatal intensive care unit.

Later, after visiting her, I left the hospital with a heavy heart and racing thoughts. I felt helpless as a mother. As I was driving away from the hospital, looking straight ahead, I had an unobstructed view of the glistening sea and the beautiful blue sky. In that moment, I was keenly aware of God's Spirit, assuring me that God is the creator of all things. Surely I could trust God to take care of my daughter, whom God had also created.

My heart lifted, and my worries turned to praise for the God who knows me, sees me and cares for me. God's presence with me strengthened my heart and shored up my faith. Even now, 40 years later, when we celebrate our daughter's birthday, I still recall that day. And I praise God all over again for being with me and with her that day and every day.

Prayer: *Dear heavenly Father, thank you for knowing us and for being with us always. Amen.*

Thought for the day: I am known, seen and cared for by God.

Amy C. (Virginia, USA)

PRAYER FOCUS: PARENTS OF BABIES IN INTENSIVE CARE

Finish well

Read 2 Timothy 4:5–8

Blessed is the one who perseveres under trial because, having stood the test, that person will receive the crown of life that the Lord has promised to those who love him.

James 1:12 (NIV)

I've run 25 marathons, and I've enjoyed and finished strong in many of them. However, some were not so enjoyable. There was one where I struggled with considerable pain and fatigue and wondered if I could finish the race. At the 18-mile mark, I was in so much pain that I had to slow my pace and take short breaks. But I received encouragement from one of the course volunteers and other runners experiencing similar struggles. To finish the race, I needed inner strength, determination, endurance and perseverance.

When I eventually crossed the finish line, my doubts and thoughts of the struggles, aches and pains vanished. A finisher's medal was placed around my neck. Even though I was in pain, I was glad that I had persevered to finish the race.

The course of life and our spiritual journey can be like running a marathon – at times enjoyable and at others full of difficulties and uncertainties. But with the Holy Spirit moving in us and the strength God gives, we can persevere. Then, as we draw near to life's finish line, the struggles, pains and disappointments we experienced will fade as we look to our reward – the crown of life – in heaven.

Prayer: *Dear heavenly Father, grant us strength to keep the faith, and help us to persevere as we journey with you. Amen.*

Thought for the day: God gives me the strength to persevere.

Donald Wollenhaupt (Georgia, USA)

 PRAYER FOCUS: THOSE WHO ENCOURAGE AND SUPPORT ME

In God's hands

Read Isaiah 42:5–9

I am the Lord; I have called you in righteousness; I have taken you by the hand and kept you.

Isaiah 42:6 (NRSV)

In my work with adults with developmental disabilities, I spend part of my time in the wood workshop. Often I sit next to Luca, who loves to sand wooden spoons. Sometimes he starts to rub across the grain of the wood, rather than with it. Then I reach out my hand and gently redirect him. Sometimes he becomes preoccupied with rubbing one spot over and over, missing the edges and corners. Again, I take his hand and hold it in the place that still needs attention. If Luca didn't trust me, our collaboration would turn into a struggle. But with trust and respect for each other, we are able to make something beautiful.

Isaiah's words about the divine call to righteousness remind me of my work with Luca. God wants to take us by the hand, not because we can't do anything ourselves but because sometimes we need a bit of guidance or redirection to make our efforts more effective. God wants to teach us, giving us helpful limits while we are still finding our way. Trusting in God who takes us by the hand is what turns our activity into righteousness, producing fruits that are beautiful, true and good.

Prayer: *Dear Lord, help us to walk in your ways. May your hand guide, redirect and focus us as we participate in your work of love. Amen.*

Thought for the day: I will trust God's hand to guide me in the way I should go.

Lory Widmer Hess (Bern, Switzerland)

Where God leads

Read Acts 9:10–19

Make me to know your ways, O Lord; teach me your paths.

Psalm 25:4 (NRSV)

One winter morning as I was walking to the church where I am the pastor, I thought of an older couple that lived down the street and wondered if they would like to attend some upcoming church activities. At the end of their slippery driveway was a newspaper, which I picked up and brought to their front door.

My neighbour was pleasantly surprised to see me, and she invited me inside for some tea. I was able to sit with her and her husband for a while. As we drank tea and chatted, she said, 'God is good', explaining that she had been wondering how she would get the newspaper. She went on to describe her feelings of loneliness and told me that she believed God had sent me to cheer her up.

What I did wasn't much. I just stopped by a neighbour's house, gave them their newspaper, delivered a church newsletter and stayed to chat. However, we both believed that God's hand was at work. I was grateful to know my neighbours better and especially to feel that God had used me as an instrument of God's love. We never know how and when God might use us, so let us always be open to the movement of the Holy Spirit in our lives.

Prayer: *Holy Spirit, we thank you for leading and guiding us. Help us to be open to your promptings and to be instruments of God's love wherever we go. In Jesus' name we pray. Amen.*

Thought for the day: I will be open to where God leads me today.

Rebecca L. T. Cho (Massachusetts, USA)

 PRAYER FOCUS: ELDERLY PEOPLE IN MY COMMUNITY

God is with us

Read Hebrews 11:1–16

Come near to God and he will come near to you.

James 4:8 (NIV)

I was at a loss and feeling depressed as I finished a difficult freshman year of college. I had dreamed of becoming a doctor, but I had failed a class and lost my scholarship. Then at the end-of-semester gathering of my choir, we selected slips of paper with Bible verses on them from a basket. I got James 4:8, and I took it to heart.

That summer I volunteered at a camp ministry, where I was more than assured that God was still with me. In the forests, fields and creek, while working to make a difference in kids' lives, God met me. I knew that God was still very real and attentive to my situation.

Hebrews 11:6 emphasises the importance of faith: 'Without faith it is impossible to please God.' And the whole of Hebrews 11 offers the encouragement of those who have gone before us, responding in faith to God. Times of closeness with God encourage us to look ahead in hope, knowing that there is a God 'who is able to do immeasurably more than all we ask or imagine, according to his power that is at work within us' (Ephesians 3:20).

Prayer: *Dear God, give us hope and faith so that we may reach out and embrace what you call us to, knowing that you are always with us. Amen.*

Thought for the day: Even when I feel lost, God knows where I am.

Nathaniel Lawrence (Oregon, USA)

No less

Read Luke 15:3–6

'When he has found [the lost sheep], he lays it on his shoulders and rejoices.'

Luke 15:5 (NRSV)

My oldest grandson, Judah, was the only grandchild for four years. During this time, he received lots of attention. Then along came Addison. Although he loved his new cousin, Judah did not understand how I could love them both. Sometimes when I cared for Addison he whispered, 'But, Nannie, I thought you loved me.'

Recently I came across a picture of a stranded lamb drenched in the pouring rain and Jesus running towards it. The caption was the story of Jesus leaving the 99 to find the one. Although I have heard the story several times, this visual elicited a new emotional reaction from me. It reminded me that God loves each person the same. God's love is not greater for the Christian or the good-deed doer than it is for those who do not follow Christ.

When things do not go my way, I am quick to whisper, 'But, God, I thought you loved me.' My love for Judah is no less than my love for Addison. God's love for someone else does not change God's love for me. Everyone receives the same unconditional love.

Prayer: *Dear God, help us to share your love with others and not to be judgemental. In Jesus' name. Amen.*

Thought for the day: Love others like Jesus.

Denise (Iris) M. Greene (North Carolina, USA)

My home

Read Zephaniah 3:14–20

'At that time I will gather you; at that time I will bring you home. I will give you honour and praise among all the peoples of the earth when I restore your fortunes before your very eyes,' says the Lord.

Zephaniah 3:20 (NIV)

Hopping from one place to another, I moved between the homes of my friends and relatives as I struggled to find employment in a city far from home. Grappling with financial lack and the overwhelming sense of being a burden, I couldn't help but be embarrassed, especially when I had to prolong my stay for months. I wondered if I was overstaying my welcome, even though my hosts were gracious. I longed for a place to call my own.

However, my deep sense of grief and loneliness was met with comfort as I read about God's promise to the Israelites to bring them back to their homeland. God would remove their shame, and the scattered people would return to their beautiful land and enjoy its produce. They would feel safe and secure. This hope would grant them the strength to endure hardships and fill them with peace as they waited upon the Lord.

As I wait for God to bring me to my physical home, I trust God to be my spiritual home – my comfort and shelter. I rest in God's loving embrace.

Prayer: *Dear God, we trust someday you will bring us home to a place where we can lie safely. And no matter where we are, we thank you for being a home for us all. Amen.*

Thought for the day: Wherever I am, God is my home.

Elina Yeptho (Nagaland, India)

Strength to soar

Read Isaiah 40:26–31

But those who hope in the Lord will renew their strength; they will fly up on wings like eagles; they will run and not be tired; they will walk and not be weary.

Isaiah 40:31 (CEB)

Recently, I underwent surgery for a minor heart attack. The trauma left me very shocked and having little strength of my own. My days were filled with fear, worry and anxiety, leaving me feeling weak.

One Sunday I visited my local church, where one of the elders read out the above verse to the congregation. The scripture filled me with hope and a desire to trust God and his power. An eagle will not fly very far if it has to flap its wings too much, using up all its energy. Instead, by using wind thermals, especially from storms, they can soar.

I realised that in the midst of my own storm, I had been flapping my wings, trying to achieve everything in my own strength. We were never created to handle the weight of life on our own; we were made to depend on God and his strength.

I decided, therefore, to start praying once a week with a friend. A few weeks later, I attended a Bible study group. And weeks after that, I attended morning prayer at my local church. Slowly I began to experience God's grace in my weakness and in ways I never would have in my own strength.

Prayer: *Lord, help us to put our hope in you, the source of our strength. Amen.*

Thought for the day: The Lord gives power to the tired and revives the exhausted (see v. 29).

Angela Uboroi (United Kingdom)

 PRAYER FOCUS: THOSE RECOVERING FROM SURGERY

Contentment

Read Philippians 4:10–13

Keep your lives free from the love of money and be content with what you have, because God has said, 'Never will I leave you; never will I forsake you.'

Hebrews 13:5 (NIV)

During the school holidays I offered to take my two young grandchildren to the botanical gardens for an outing. We planned to purchase some ice cream to eat as we walked. My grandchildren were excited about this plan, but when we got to the shop we discovered that they had no little tubs of ice cream and the ones on sticks were far too expensive. I explained to the children that we would have to wait and have ice cream another time. They both took the disappointment well and cheerfully continued with the day.

We had a fun time walking along the paths in the garden, getting a bit lost and laughing a lot. It made me think how often I have grumbled and become disappointed or angry when God didn't give me what I wanted. I learned a lesson that day from my grandchildren that contentment with God's will is the way to happiness. Even when things don't turn out the way we expect them to, we can trust God – who is always with us – for a good outcome.

Prayer: *Dear Lord, help us to be content with your plans. Help us to trust you even when we are disappointed or don't understand your purposes. May we experience the blessing of contentment. Amen.*

Thought for the day: To be content with life is a great gift.

Valerie Clark (KwaZulu-Natal, South Africa)

Greatest calling

Read 2 Corinthians 3:13–18

We all, who with unveiled faces contemplate the Lord's glory, are being transformed into his image with ever-increasing glory, which comes from the Lord, who is the Spirit.

2 Corinthians 3:18 (NIV)

I paused along the edge of the pond during my morning walk to take a picture of the blue heron that stood motionless among the reeds and grasses. A perfect mirror image of the heron was reflected on the surface of the water. The reflection was radiant in the early morning light and reminded me of how we are called to reflect the image of Christ to the world.

When I was a new Christian, I thought I needed a special talent or ability to be able to make Christ known to others. However, as I studied the Bible, I learned that it is the Holy Spirit who makes Christ known by transforming us to be more like him in holiness, grace and love (see Romans 8:29). As we cooperate with the Spirit's work, we mirror Christ through our words and actions, reflecting the character of Christ and shining his light to the world around us.

Prayer: *Thank you, O Christ, for giving us the incredible privilege of reflecting your image. May the light of your Holy Spirit shine brightly in us and through us. We pray as you taught us, 'Father, hallowed be your name, your kingdom come. Give us each day our daily bread. Forgive us our sins, for we also forgive everyone who sins against us. And lead us not into temptation' (Luke 11:2–4, NIV). Amen.*

Thought for the day: The Holy Spirit empowers me to reflect Christ's light to the world.

Ina Cochran (Pennsylvania, USA)

Like Esau

Read Genesis 33:1–9

Esau said, 'I have enough, my brother; keep what you have for yourself.'

Genesis 33:9 (NRSV)

In high school I truly felt abandoned. My parents had been divorced for many years, and financial support from my dad was rare. My mum was the sole provider for our family and did her best to make ends meet. In a desperate bid to lighten her load I went in search of my dad, hoping he would give me money for lunch or bus fare. When I finally found him, he told me he had given everything to my half sibling and turned out his empty pockets. The disappointment and sense of abandonment hit me hard. As tears rolled down my cheeks, I walked away feeling angry and empty.

However, during my devotional time a passage from Genesis 33 resonated deeply with me. In verse 9, Esau tells his brother Jacob that he has enough. I realised that even though Jacob stole Esau's blessing from their father, God had provided abundantly for Esau.

I came to understand that God's hands are always full and God's pockets are never empty. God always has more than enough for us. Now I am filled with gratitude for having much more than my dad could have given me. In moments of disappointment and abandonment, I've learned to trust in God's abundant provision.

Prayer: *Dear God, thank you for your faithfulness and loving kindness, which you pour out on us every day. Remind us that you always have enough for us. Amen.*

Thought for the day: All I have needed God's hand has provided.

Jennifer Lovelace (Kingston, Jamaica)

The table is set

Read Matthew 25:31–46

'I was hungry and you gave me something to eat, I was thirsty and you gave me something to drink, I was a stranger and you invited me in.'
Matthew 25:35 (NIV)

I remember one time when I was at my great-grandmother's house for supper. She stood next to her old table, which consumed the kitchen and was filled with favourite foods and plates for everyone. 'Supper is ready; come to the table,' she exclaimed in a tone of readiness and love.

The old floors creaked as everyone hurried to find their seat. As we all laughed, talked and enjoyed the food, a small child asked, 'Grandma, who is this empty chair and plate for? Did you put too many plates out?' My great-grandmother smiled and answered, 'That empty chair and plate are there in case someone stops by and is hungry. We should always be prepared to welcome and feed those in need.'

Just as Matthew 25:35 encourages us to do, my great-grandmother was ready to feed a hungry traveller, neighbour or friend. Jesus also wants us to come to the table and be filled. God's table always has an open spot, and any who accept God's invitation will be filled with God's love, mercy and grace. Come to the table and be filled.

Prayer: *Dear Jesus, help us to remember and care for those who need to be fed, loved and encouraged. Thank you for setting a place at your table for each of us. Amen.*

Thought for the day: With open arms, I will welcome those who need to be fed.

Fran Marie Campbell (Indiana, USA)

What really matters

Read Hebrews 10:19–25

Let us consider how we may spur one another on towards love and good deeds.
Hebrews 10:24 (NIV)

Many years ago, I attended a children's football game. A large, open field provided plenty of area for the game but also plenty of sideline space for spectators.

As I watched the game, I noticed two dynamics at play. First, while the children were young enough that some of their football skills were rough around the edges, they were also old enough to understand the game. Running, kicking, scoring! The children played like they meant it! The second dynamic had little to do with the skill of the players. It was how everyone came together. A sense of camaraderie among spectators and players allowed everyone to cheer for everyone else.

Who ended up with the most goals wasn't all that important. All the people involved mattered – and so did all of their efforts! It should be the same in our churches and communities. The 'scorecard' of who has or who does the most isn't what's important. We can freely cheer for one another – giving support and encouragement wherever, however and to whoever needs it.

Prayer: *Dear heavenly Father, thank you for the privilege of being a part of the body of Christ. Lead us to work together for the good of all your children. In Jesus' name. Amen.*

Thought for the day: Every effort to encourage and support one another matters.

Tyler Myers (Ohio, USA)

PRAYER FOCUS: FOR UNITY IN THE BODY OF CHRIST

Something good

Read Ephesians 2:1–10

We are God's handiwork, created in Christ Jesus to do good works, which God prepared in advance for us to do.

Ephesians 2:10 (NIV)

Recently I noticed a multicoloured ball of yarn in my yarn collection. It looked too ragged for any good use, but instead of throwing it away I decided to try crocheting something with it. The result surprised me! I followed the instructions and wound up with a warm woollen hat of beautiful colours – a perfect fit.

Some things in life can be just like that scruffy yarn: poor quality and apparently without purpose. At times, our life experiences can get us down and cause us to lose perspective. But here is where the hand of the creator comes in. God is willing to make something incredible from whatever we have to offer. The Bible assures us: 'We know that in all things God works for the good of those who love him, who have been called according to his purpose' (Romans 8:28).

Because of who God is, God can bring good from anything. May we never doubt the skill of God's hand who can creatively use what we offer for the good of the world.

Prayer: *Creative God, we surrender to you all the pieces of our lives. Thank you for transforming them into something good. Amen.*

Thought for the day: Even what I deem to be useless, God can turn into good.

Carol Westerlund (Uusimaa, Finland)

Be still

Read Psalm 46:1–7, 10

'Be still, and know that I am God; I will be exalted among the nations, I will be exalted in the earth.'

Psalm 46:10 (NIV)

I was resting in a hospital bed after giving birth to our second child. I was tired, sore and very hungry; it was 10 o'clock at night, and I had not eaten all day. At least I had been able to hold my baby girl for a few minutes in the delivery room, and she looked perfect! But as the minutes ticked away, I began to feel anxious: *They should have brought her to me by now. What if something has happened? What is going on?* I searched for the call button, but it was out of reach. As panic washed over me, Psalm 46:10 came to my mind.

I realised I just needed to be still and seek God's presence in that moment. I took several deep breaths, closed my eyes and the most amazingly peaceful feeling came over me. I felt God's presence in a way I had never felt before. I knew then that God was with me and that whatever might happen, I would be all right because God was there.

My daughter was fine, but I will always remember those few moments as transformational in my walk of faith. If we seek to be still in God's presence when we are challenged by life's unexpected or delayed events, we will know God's peace beyond our understanding.

Prayer: *Dear God, help us always to know that you are ever-present in our lives. In trust, we open ourselves to you. In the name of Jesus we pray. Amen.*

Thought for the day: God's peaceful presence can help me in moments of anxiety.

Tamala Dykes Paxton (Delaware, USA)

Beloved community

Read Galatians 3:23–29

In Christ Jesus you are all children of God through faith.

Galatians 3:26 (NRSV)

In 1955, when I was 11, my mum and I spent the autumn at the home of Dr Abbie Clement Jackson, my 'adoptive' grandmother. Her neighbourhood, my Boy Scout troop, my church and my school were African American. When the local school district wanted to bus me 20 minutes away to a white school, Grandma Abbie and Mum convinced the superintendent that I would be more comfortable remaining at the school where I had friends.

One morning, Grandma Abbie asked me to greet her escort who would be walking her to the African Methodist Episcopal church conference where she was the keynote speaker. Her escort was the Revd Dr Martin Luther King Jr.

That afternoon, Dr King and his parents came back to the house for tea and conversation. At one point, Dr King asked me, 'What is it like being the only white boy in an all Negro school?' I thought for a moment about my community and said, 'It's normal.'

The Beloved Community Dr King spoke of begins when we feel comfortable in our skin while respecting the person next to us. When we look into one another's eyes and see a child of God, we find community.

Prayer: *Gracious God, may your love for us manifest itself in our love for others. Amen.*

Thought for the day: Community is formed when we recognise God in one another.

David Russell (Illinois, USA)

 PRAYER FOCUS: TO SEE ALL PEOPLE AS CHILDREN OF GOD

Keep praying

Read Luke 18:1–8

Elijah was a human being, even as we are. He prayed earnestly that it would not rain, and it did not rain on the land for three and a half years. Again he prayed, and the heavens gave rain, and the earth produced its crops.

James 5:17–18 (NIV)

When I arrived for dinner with a new friend from church, she introduced me to another guest, 'Come and meet Kathleen.' As I entered the lounge I was surprised to find an elderly woman I had not seen in years. Her sparkling blue eyes met mine, and with tears of joyful recognition, we embraced.

Despite the time that had passed and her changed appearance, I still recognised this wonderful woman. She had regularly visited my family after my father had left us. Whenever she visited, she brought thoughtful little gifts and was genuinely interested in my brother and me. I loved the sense of peace she always embodied.

Now, almost three decades since we last saw each other, I discovered that she was a Christian and had prayed constantly for my family to come to Christ. My mother, brother and I had since committed our lives to Christ, and I believe Kathleen's prayers played a big part in making that happen.

Sometimes we see the results of our prayers, and other times we don't. But we are encouraged to keep praying and trust the outcome to God.

Prayer: *Dear Lord, help us to keep on praying, trusting that you hear us and are at work, even when we don't perceive it. Amen.*

Thought for the day: I will pray and trust God with the outcome.

Miki Parsons (England, United Kingdom)

In any circumstance

Read Psalm 34:1–14

I will praise you, Lord my God, with all my heart; I will glorify your name forever.

Psalm 86:12 (NIV)

My wife and I were on a much-needed vacation, hiking the mountains and canyons of northern Arizona. We had gone through several months of challenging times, and the fresh air and beautiful scenery were refreshing for mind, body and soul.

On one hike, I noticed a small cedar tree growing on the side of a rocky outcropping. I stopped and examined it. There was very little dirt at the base of the tree – it looked like it was growing right out of the rock. Despite living in a very challenging environment, the tree survived and grew.

Like that tree, we aren't always in control of our circumstances. Surely the little tree, if able to choose its location, would have picked a spot with fertile soil and adequate sunlight and rainfall. But it didn't have the power to make that choice. Instead, it was fulfilling its purpose of growing, even in the challenging environment in which it found itself. Shouldn't we do the same? We were made to glorify God. Let us serve our purpose, regardless of location or circumstance.

Prayer: *Heavenly Father, thank you for creating us. No matter where we find ourselves, may our hearts, words and actions glorify you always. Amen.*

Thought for the day: I will praise and worship God regardless of my circumstances.

Clint Taylor (Illinois, USA)

You are shining

Read Matthew 5:13–16

Let your light so shine before men, that they may see your good works, and glorify your Father which is in heaven.

Matthew 5:16 (KJV)

While I was taking care of a patient one day, he said to me, ‘You are shining in this place.’ I looked at him in awe. Every day I prayed that Jesus Christ’s light would shine through me so that others would see him. This patient had no idea that this was my prayer, but his comment felt like confirmation that God had heard me and answered my prayer. After hearing his words, I felt the joy of knowing that God had worked through me.

In Matthew 5:14–16, Jesus says, ‘Ye are the light of the world. A city that is set on an hill cannot be hid. Neither do men light a candle, and put it under a bushel… Let your light so shine before men, that they may see your good works, and glorify your Father which is in heaven.’ We live in a world that is filled with darkness, and as Christians we are to show others the way to Jesus. We are to represent Christ wherever we are. That day I realised that no matter our circumstances we can be the light of Jesus Christ, brightening the places where we find ourselves.

Prayer: *Dear Lord, may your light shine in us so that others can see you. In Jesus’ name we pray. Amen.*

Thought for the day: Jesus’ light shines through me to others when I focus on him.

Teresa Milsap (Mississippi, USA)

In God's presence

Read Psalm 84

Even the sparrow has found a home, and the swallow a nest for herself, where she may have her young – a place near your altar, Lord Almighty, my King and my God. Blessed are those who dwell in your house; they are ever praising you.

Psalm 84:3–4 (NIV)

One evening I needed to update the sign by the front door of the church where I was serving. We had been meeting in the church basement lately, so the entryway had largely been left unused.

As I started my task, I heard loud protests from a nearby bird. I didn't pay much attention at first, but then suddenly a robin swooped at me. That got my attention! Looking up, I saw a nest tucked above the nearby light fixture with three baby birds in it. I quickly finished up and left them in peace.

Looking at the robin's nest I remembered Psalm 84, a song of praise for the gift of God's presence in the temple. It notes that even the birds can find a home near the altar of the Lord. Gathering for worship reminds us of God's presence with us. Our places of worship can serve as reminders of God's grace, forgiveness, faithfulness and empowering Spirit as we go into the world.

As I left the family of robins, I reflected: *Do I delight in God's presence? Have I built my home by God's altar? How might I invite others to know the blessing of God's presence?*

Prayer: *Ever-present God, help us to be aware of your presence wherever we are and to build our lives in you. May we delight in your goodness and grace. Amen.*

Thought for the day: What places help me connect to God's presence?

Megan P. (Ontario, Canada)

Real and unrehearsed

Read Luke 22:39–46

During his days on earth, Christ offered prayers and requests with loud cries and tears.

Hebrews 5:7 (CEB)

If my son is running around our house and hurts himself, he will cry out. And if it hurts a lot, he may cry out with tears. My son doesn't have to try to calm down and then tell me in an even voice, 'Father, I wish to inform you that I have a problem.' No! He can cry out, and I will hear and answer.

Sometimes we think that when we bring our pain or distressing circumstances to God we must try to calm down first and then tell God how we feel. But when Jesus prayed in the garden on the night he was betrayed, our reading tells us that he was in 'anguish' and that he prayed so fervently he sweat blood. Jesus didn't put his prayer through an emotional filter; in a prayer that was honest, earnest and unrehearsed, he said, 'Father, if you are willing, take this cup away from me.'

Like Jesus, when we are experiencing extreme stress and anxiety – a terminal illness, a loved one has died, our spouse wants a divorce – we can turn to God with prayers that are emotionally raw and unfiltered, knowing that God hears our cries and sees our tears.

Prayer: *Thank you, Father God, that we can come to you honestly in moments of pain and sorrow, pouring out our whole heart to you. Amen.*

Thought for the day: Prayer is unrehearsed communication with God.

Jeremy K. Mullen (Pennsylvania, USA)

Always in sight

Read John 10:11–18

You [Lord] know when I sit and when I rise; you perceive my thoughts from afar.

Psalm 139:2 (NIV)

While looking through old photos, I came across one taken when I had gone to a family reunion with my then fiancé, Tom. Everyone was gathered for a family photo, and I was standing in the group beside Tom. At the last moment, realising that I was not 'officially' family, I quickly stepped aside. In the photo, people are facing forward, toward the photographer – all except Tom. He's turned sideways, watching after me. After 53 years of marriage, I look at that photo and smile. All these years later, I am still blessed by a husband who is lovingly focused on me.

As wonderful as this is, scripture tells me that I have an even greater blessing. I have a heavenly Father who watches over my 'coming and going both now and forevermore' (Psalm 121:8). This is an assurance to all who trust God. Even in difficult times or times without the support of others, we are never alone. Regardless of life's circumstances, each of us can know that God sees us and cares for us with an everlasting love.

Prayer: *Dear Father, thank you for blessing us with your caring presence. Help us to know that you are present with us in all the times of our lives. Amen.*

Thought for the day: God always sees and always cares.

Sandra Sullivan (West Virginia, USA)

Dependence

Read Ecclesiastes 4:9–12

If they fall, one will lift up the other, but woe to one who is alone and falls and does not have another to help.

Ecclesiastes 4:10 (NRSV)

In our modern times, many cultures promote the importance of being independent and self-reliant. Independence is considered a vital character trait and is something we stubbornly hang on to, even when we grow older or face difficulties or physical limitations.

When I was younger, I was proud of my ability to do things well on my own. I did not think I needed to rely on others or that it might even be important to seek assistance. However, years of physical limitations have taught me to value dependence rather than independence.

God said in Genesis 2:18: 'It is not good that the man should be alone; I will make him a helper as his partner.' God identified the need for humans to help and depend on one another. This is not to suggest we should expect others to do everything for us. It just means we would do well to admit when we need help and, most important, ask for and accept that help. Perhaps in the future, we could all value dependence a little more than independence.

Prayer: *Father God, thank you for those who help us when we cannot manage alone. May we be willing to accept help and offer help to others. Amen.*

Thought for the day: God created us to depend on one another.

Bronwyn Ashton Winch (Queensland, Australia)

PRAYER FOCUS: SOMEONE EXPERIENCING LOSS OF INDEPENDENCE

Second chances

Read Psalm 18:1–5

In my distress I called upon the Lord; to my God I cried for help. From his temple he heard my voice, and my cry to him reached his ears.
Psalm 18:6 (NRSV)

When I was younger, my brother and I loved playing video games. Often the games had the option to restart after we expended the 'lives' we started out with. We had a second chance to move forward and to apply the knowledge we had gained about the obstacles we would face.

I never realised that there could be second chances in life until God showed me a way to escape the entangling grasp of alcoholism. Those who suffer from or know someone suffering from this affliction of mind and body may understand the feeling of hopelessness and peril I had felt. But the grace of God showed me a second chance. Psalm 18:1–6 reminds me of the love God has for me and of how God's strength helped me to overcome the seemingly insurmountable obstacles of addiction.

Scriptures like Psalm 18 and Numbers 6:24–26 remind me of the second chances we have through Jesus. Now I happily seize every second chance that I have in this new life to be a vessel of love, peace, hope and joy – step by step, one day at a time.

Prayer: *Faithful God, thank you for opportunities to use the blessings of knowledge that you have provided through our past experiences. In your name we humbly pray. Amen.*

Thought for the day: I will embrace every new opportunity to be a vessel of God's love and hope.

Ken M. (New Hampshire, USA)

No words

Read 2 Corinthians 1:1–11

Let your conversation be always full of grace, seasoned with salt, so that you may know how to answer everyone.
Colossians 4:6 (NIV)

Just before Christmas, my best friend Sandra's husband, Doug, died of a sudden heart attack at only 59 years old. Sandra was devastated.

I found that Doug's death brought back memories of my own bereavement years ago, but my thoughts were now all on Sandra. Their family lived far away, so as soon as I heard the news, I went to sit with her while we waited for family to arrive. She was perched on the edge of the sofa wiping her eyes, sometimes sobbing, sometimes just staring out the window in a frozen state. *What could I say?* Everything I could think to say sounded trite and inappropriate. No words of comfort sounded right. So I just sat beside her with my arm around her shoulder. She seemed hardly aware of my presence.

I stayed for a few hours, occasionally making a drink or sandwich, though she barely touched them, and I hardly uttered a word. I joined her grieving as she waited for her family to arrive and for the bustle of funeral arrangements to intrude on her grief. After the funeral, she said to me, 'Thank you for just sitting with me. I didn't need your words, only your presence.'

Prayer: *Loving Lord, we thank you for being the ultimate comforter for those who grieve. Guide us to comfort those who mourn. Amen.*

Thought for the day: My presence can comfort those who grieve; no words are needed.

Carol Purves (England, United Kingdom)

All seasons

Read Psalm 16:1–7

I bless the Lord, who gives me counsel; in the night also my heart instructs me.

Psalm 16:7 (NRSV)

Where I live, we have a shrub called an azalea. Azaleas have beautiful blooms in early spring, thrive in partial shade, and grow quite large if not trimmed. They tend to go unnoticed the majority of the year, simply looking like a dark green shrub. But in the early spring, beautiful blooms adorn azaleas with bright colours that are pleasing to the eye.

Thinking of the way azaleas go unnoticed, I wondered how many times we go through the year not noticing the grace and love of Jesus – only to realise during the Christmas and Easter seasons what Christ means to us and how his grace and love makes us feel. Let us be mindful not to let our Lord and Saviour ever go unnoticed. Jesus' grace and love have no boundaries. His love for us is constant and never-ending!

Prayer: *Lord Jesus, help us to remember that your love, mercy and grace are intentional and never-ending. Give us the desire to worship and study your word all year long. Amen.*

Thought for the day: I will remember Jesus' grace and love in all seasons.

JB Zahn (Florida, USA)

God cares

Read 1 Peter 5:6–7

'The Lord himself goes before you and will be with you; he will never leave you nor forsake you. Do not be afraid; do not be discouraged.'
Deuteronomy 31:8 (NIV)

In early May 2010, our town received more than 15 inches of rain over several days, causing significant flooding around the city. Unfortunately, our home was affected by the flooding. The seemingly impossible task of repairing our home and the devastation in the town were almost more than we could bear. We wondered where God was and how God could turn this tragedy into something good. Fear and anxiety quickly set in. But as we prayed and sought God's guidance, God not only brought restoration to our home but blessed us with people along the way to help with the rebuilding process. Something that had once seemed impossible was now possible with God.

When adversity makes us feel hopeless and overwhelmed, it is best to turn to God and trust in God's plan. God cares for each of us and about the things that trouble us – big or small. Letting go of worry and allowing God to lead us through requires trust, but doing so gives us peace and comfort when we need it most.

Prayer: *Dear God, help us to hand over to you the things that make us anxious, knowing you care for us and will provide what we need. Amen.*

Thought for the day: I will trust God when I am troubled.

Tracy Martin (Tennessee, USA)

PRAYER FOCUS: THOSE FEELING HOPELESS AND OVERWHELMED

One who serves

Read Luke 22:24–30

'Who is greater, the one who is at the table or the one who serves? Is it not the one at the table? But I am among you as one who serves.'
Luke 22:27 (NRSV)

As a homemaker and mother to a toddler, I always seem to put myself last – last to eat, last to bathe, last to sleep, etc. From the moment I wake up, I take care of my child, prepare and serve meals, and look after the needs of our household. And because I am nursing, mothering continues through the night for me.

Motherhood has both challenged and clarified my view of service. Honestly, when I look at the housework I still need to do or when my child needs me right as I finally sit down to eat, I can't help but feel a bit lonely in my service.

However, one day when I was almost ready to succumb to my feelings of insignificance, I read Luke 22. When a dispute arose among the disciples about who was the greatest among them, Jesus revealed what it means to follow him. He said, 'The greatest among you must become like the youngest and the leader like one who serves… I am among you as one who serves' (vv. 26–27). Right when I thought I was alone in my service, I encountered this truth – Jesus is with me. And I am following his example when I serve others.

Prayer: *Lord Jesus, thank you for your example of service. Help us to serve like you, and give us joy as we do. Amen.*

Thought for the day: I follow the example of Jesus when I serve others.

Quennie Joyce Ibarra (Misamis Occidental, Philippines)

The new and the old

Read Psalm 104:10–18

Thou renewest the face of the earth.

Psalm 104:1 (NRSV)

Nature is the best recycling system I know. It does not discard old material. As I go walking in the woodland near where I live, I see the old and the new live alongside each other. Both new and old trees are all around me – the living trees with their fresh growth stretching up to the light, while the fallen leaves, branches and trees lie rotting at my feet.

Every growing tree is a vibrant engine of new life, soon to be home for nesting birds as well as providing food like grubs and caterpillars for hatchlings. Yet the dying trees are creating new life too by enriching the soil to nourish new growth, and their dead wood is alive with tiny mites and spiders. Here truly is the glory of God's creation – God's cycle of life with its clear message of renewal and hope for the coming year and beyond.

As we say goodbye to January, how are your new year's resolutions holding up? Yes, with the new year comes the prospect of new beginnings, but surely it is also a natural time to look back, to review the old year and perhaps search for new ideas in the plans that did not work out. Maybe we can find green shoots in old bulbs.

Prayer: *Father God, thank you for forgiving us for our past sins, and help us to look ahead with faith and hope. Amen.*

Thought for the day: Jesus Christ is the same yesterday, today and forever (see Hebrews 13:8).

D. Carole Wilsher (Wales, United Kingdom)

Never-ending grace

Read 2 Corinthians 12:9–10

He said to me, 'My grace is sufficient for you, for my power is made perfect in weakness.'

2 Corinthians 12:9 (NIV)

When my husband was diagnosed with ALS, we faced a decision: would we dwell on the negative and challenging aspects or make each day the best day possible, knowing that the next one would not be easier? It was a difficult and heartbreaking journey as he was slowly stripped of the ability to perform daily tasks – eventually even walking, eating, sleeping and breathing. However, even on the darkest days, we experienced God's sustaining grace in remarkable ways.

During this time, I was gifted a journal titled 'Grace'. Initially, I rejected the idea of recording my days, as my time and energy were consumed with caretaking. But then, as day after day we saw God's goodness and grace, I decided to keep a journal of thanks for God's guidance, protection and love throughout our journey. I made bulleted lists of the compassion and love bestowed on us. I noted the help we received unloading my husband's walker – and later his power wheelchair – as we arrived for Sunday worship, the home-repair services done at no charge, and the food that a friend delivered to us weekly for over a year.

These acts of compassion and love reminded us of the promise of God's everlasting love. Indeed, God's grace is more than sufficient. It's life-changing and extraordinary.

Prayer: *Dear Lord, we thank you for the promise of your endless grace and for the ways we see it manifested in our daily lives. Amen.*

Thought for the day: When I notice God's grace in my life, I find peace.

LaDonna Marshall (Oklahoma, USA)

It takes time

Read Acts 1:1–5

He gave them this command: 'Do not leave Jerusalem, but wait for the gift my Father promised.'

Acts 1:4 (NIV)

When my brother Einar and I were small, our mother sometimes needed to distract us when we were a little too noisy. If she needed to concentrate, she gave us each an egg in two bowls, gave us forks and a dash of sugar, and told us to whip eggnog – we both loved eggnog!

Have you ever tried to whip eggnog with a fork? Let me tell you, it takes time! A lot of time! I remember that we would sit on the kitchen floor and start whipping. Finally, when we had our eggnog, we ate it with great satisfaction. 'Sometimes it takes time to get something good', Mum said to us. She knew how to motivate us to stick with a time-consuming task.

In our spiritual life it is also a good thing to have patience and wait for the Lord's timing. Jesus told his disciples that they should 'wait for the gift my Father promised' – the Holy Spirit. My thoughts go also to Ecclesiastes 11:1 – 'Send out your bread upon the waters, for after many days you will get it back' (NRSV). When we persevere with patience and faithfulness, we will see God's provision at work in our lives.

Prayer: *Loving Saviour, open our hearts and help us patiently await your blessings. In the name of Jesus, we pray. Amen.*

Thought for the day: The Lord's timetable is different than mine.

Øystein Brinch (Vestfold, Norway)

More than enough

Read Matthew 20:1–16

'Are you envious because I am generous?'
Matthew 20:15 (NRSV)

One of my kids has an innate sense of fairness. He can be counted on to divvy up snacks so that everyone gets their fair share. When it comes to chores, he insists that if he cleared the table then it is only fair that his sister should do the dishes.

I tend to gravitate towards a strict sense of fairness too. However, when I reflect on it, I realise that the 'fair' approach is often based on certain limiting factors: the kids take turns because there is only one jump rope; we portion out the strawberries because there are only a handful left. But what if there were an abundance of strawberries? What if there were unlimited scooters, jump ropes and trampolines for all the kids? Who would worry about the number of berries each child ate or how many minutes each child played with a toy? We wouldn't – because there would be more than enough.

It's easy for me to resonate with what feels like the unfair treatment of the first, early-morning workers in Jesus' parable of the workers in the vineyard. They received the same pay as those who had worked only a few hours, and it doesn't seem fair. But the answer Jesus gives doesn't focus on fairness. Instead, he points out the generosity of our Father God. God's grace is inexhaustible and abundant. God always gives us more than enough.

Prayer: *Dear God, thank you for the gift of your grace, which you lavishly pour out on us. Help us to show grace to the people we encounter today and every day. Amen.*

Thought for the day: There is an abundance of grace, and God gives it generously.

Ree Pashley (Indiana, USA)

 PRAYER FOCUS: DAY LABOURERS

God provides

Read Psalm 111

God is able to bless you abundantly, so that in all things at all times, having all that you need, you will abound in every good work.
2 Corinthians 9:8 (NIV)

Five years ago, my life was turned upside down when I became disabled from trauma I endured. At the time, I couldn't imagine how I would survive. But God provided. God brought amazing people into my life and pets to love and hug when tears streamed down my face. God provided me with shelter, food and financial resources.

Through it all, God has been with me, providing opportunities and support – and now rest. Even as I still struggle, I try to remember all that God has blessed me with. The blessings may be different than I imagined, but they still reassure me of God's love for me. My creator knows what I need better than anyone else. Honestly, I believe it took this upheaval to remind me that God is with me and always provides.

The change from who I used to be to who I am today still causes me grief. I don't know where I'll be tomorrow or years down the road, but I know God will be there. God has provided for me in the past and continues to do so. Each day I can take a few moments to reflect on the blessings God has sent, and I can trust that God will continue to provide for me and for all God's children.

Prayer: *Dear Lord, help us to see the blessings you send us and to show gratitude for your gifts. Amen.*

Thought for the day: God's love and blessings sustain me during difficult times.

Bre Stock (New York, USA)

Alone with God

Read Matthew 6:5–15

My sacrifice, O God, is a broken spirit; a broken and contrite heart you, God, will not despise.

Psalm 51:17 (NIV)

When Jesus said, 'When you pray, go into your room, close the door and pray to your Father, who is unseen' (Matthew 6:6), he was highlighting the importance of humility and the connections we can experience when we are alone with God. Away from the public eye, we can be authentic and sincere – no posturing, no masks. The Lord is not impressed with our eloquent words. Sincerity, rather than style, is important to God.

Our devotional time is indispensable for our spiritual health and is a way for us to cultivate a strong relationship with God. Time with God creates an oasis of healing, freedom, comfort and strength. It is where we feel loved, affirmed and more prepared to withstand moments of adversity and temptation. Alone with God, we can connect with our creator in a way that we cannot in public. Our prayer life is deepened when we go to God just as we are.

Prayer: *Holy God, help us seek you every day and be more intentional in prioritising time with you. We pray the prayer your Son taught us, 'Our Father which art in heaven, Hallowed be thy name. Thy kingdom come, Thy will be done in earth, as it is in heaven. Give us this day our daily bread. And forgive us our debts, as we forgive our debtors. And lead us not into temptation, but deliver us from evil: For thine is the kingdom, and the power, and the glory, for ever. Amen' (Matthew 6:9–13, KJV).*

Thought for the day: Each day is an opportunity to prioritise time with God.

Narda Vargas Guerrero (Dominican Republic)

A little cake

Read 1 Kings 17:8–16

Elijah said unto her, Fear not; go and do as thou hast said: but make me thereof a little cake first, and bring it unto me, and after make for thee and for thy son.

1 Kings 17:13 (KJV)

Sometimes God helps us in unexpected ways, just as God helped the widow in today's scripture. Perhaps when she saw Elijah she hoped that he was bringing food. Instead, he came asking *her* for a cake!

Why would God ask the woman to make a cake for a stranger when she was the one in need? Sometimes God does the same with us. We may be busy or going through a difficult time, but God brings us a neighbour in need. How do we respond? Can we give them a smile, a hug or a word of encouragement, even as we're experiencing challenges?

Elijah's request wasn't out of selfishness. He was following God's instructions. But I wonder if he felt ashamed, begging from a widow. And I wonder if she was offended by his request. Ultimately, both obeyed God, and God blessed them with food during a famine. When God asks us to share something we've saved for ourselves, let us remember the woman's obedience and trust that God can use even our small contributions to make a big difference.

Prayer: *Father God, help us to serve someone in need today and to do it with a willing and generous spirit. Amen.*

Thought for the day: I will share what I have because with it God can do great things.

Peter Caligiuri (Florida, USA)

PRAYER FOCUS: THOSE WHO SHARE GENEROUSLY WITH ME

Rest

Read Matthew 14:13–23

Jesus often withdrew to lonely places and prayed.
Luke 5:16 (NIV)

Recently, I had the opportunity to spend time with a dear friend who is experiencing a health challenge. As we discussed treatment and doctors' recommendations, I noticed that there was an emphasis on rest. We often equate rest with sleep. Sleep is a necessity, but rest isn't necessarily. We talked about what resting might look like during this time. We prayed together for a better understanding of rest and God's work in our lives.

Rest can be difficult for those of us who schedule every minute of the day. But our bodies, minds and souls thirst for rest. It is essential and fulfilling. Jesus understood and valued the concept of rest. He took time away from his ministry to be refreshed.

When we allow God to do the work of rest in us, it brings value to our daily tasks and makes our worship more meaningful. Rest is an invitation to fall into God's loving arms, letting our creator heal, nourish and hold us as we soak in God's beautiful presence.

Prayer: *Dear Father God, thank you for the gift of rest that allows us to become closer to you. Amen.*

Thought for the day: I will follow Jesus' example and take time to rest.

Nancy P. (Ohio, USA)

Determined

Read Psalm 121

Surely, Lord, you bless the righteous; you surround them with your favour as with a shield.

Psalm 5:12 (NIV)

I was riding the bus to church when I saw a woman suddenly snatch the purse of another passenger sitting close to me. I immediately prayed for God's help as the robber approached me and demanded that I give her my satchel. I felt emboldened, and it must have shown on my face. When the robber looked at me, she appeared startled and exited the bus quickly even though I had done nothing to her.

My attention then turned to what was happening to the bus driver – he was being assaulted by an apparent accomplice. I rushed to help the driver and wrestled with the accomplice, all the while praying for God to give me strength. A few moments later, the accomplice was subdued and afterward was turned over to the authorities.

As I continued on my way to church, people who had witnessed these events started applauding, though I didn't understand why. I was quick to tell them that without God's help, none of my actions would have been possible. God was my help; God was my shield.

Prayer: *Merciful God, help us to hold fast to the words of the psalmist, trusting that you will guard our going out and our coming in. Amen.*

Thought for the day: God is by my side all day, every day.

Milton Gaitán Castrillón (Valle del Cauca, Colombia)

God speaks

Read Jeremiah 29:11–13

I know the plans I have in mind for you, declares the Lord; they are plans for peace, not disaster, to give you a future filled with hope.

Jeremiah 29:11 (CEB)

I have had a wonderful life. I graduated from high school and college with honours. I served as a naval officer and later had a successful career in public relations. I had a husband and a beautiful, gifted daughter. I was a deacon and Sunday school teacher at my church.

I am also an alcoholic who lost it all. I lost my soul, my voice, my family and my God. But God didn't lose me. God never loses us. After 20 years and spending more time in a drunken stupor than conscious, God spoke to me, demanding that I pour out the alcohol and telling me that God had plans for me. With Jesus beside me, I poured all of it down the drain, and I've not had a drop of alcohol in nearly three years as I write this.

Now I'm in the process of rebuilding a relationship with my daughter, and I'm loving the bond I have with my two new grandchildren. I'm rebuilding other parts of my life too. I'm in the process of purchasing my first home. I've found strength and confidence in myself that I didn't know existed, but God did. I've come to recognise that my relationship with God is the most important one in my life. I am like the prodigal son. And through it all, Jesus has remained at my side. He's always been there, and I am forgiven.

Prayer: *Dear God, thank you for your everlasting presence in our lives. May we find strength and peace in knowing that you are with us always. Amen.*

Thought for the day: I am loved and forgiven by God.

Laurie S. (Virginia, USA)

Got a minute?

Read James 5:13–16

Confess your sins to each other and pray for each other.
James 5:16 (CEB)

I used to work with a man who I knew to be a Christian and who prayed fervently. Once when I was scheduled for a medical procedure, I asked him to put me on his prayer list. He turned to me and said, 'Got a minute?' When I said I did, he put his hand on my shoulder and prayed with and for me right then. Afterward, he explained that he developed the habit of praying in the moment when someone asked to be put on his prayer list so he would not forget. Not only did I feel better after we prayed, but this occurrence changed my prayer life as well.

If I do not make a note, I am prone to forget things, especially as I have gotten older. I have since learned that when people ask me to put them on my prayer list, if we pray right then, they know they are being prayed for and I am less likely to forget later during my daily prayers. Now when I receive a prayer request, I also respond with, 'Got a minute?'

Prayer: *Dear Lord, give us daily opportunities to pray with others. Give us the confidence and courage to pray right then and the words to speak so that they hear your voice through us. Amen.*

Thought for the day: I will pray without ceasing.

Kim Koratsky (Tennessee, USA)

Steps to life

Read Psalm 61:2–5

In God is my salvation and my glory.

Psalm 62:7 (KJV)

In our church's praise book there is a song entitled 'Tiap Langkahku diatur oleh Tuhan'. This song is a translation of the song 'Each Step I Take'. Usually I interpret the words this way: 'Every step I take is governed by God, and his loving hand leads me.' I recall God's guidance at important times in my life. I thank God for my work, my family, and all that we experience together.

But as my husband and I get older, and our physical strength is no longer what it used to be, I interpret the words 'every step I take' as truly physical. When my husband and I walk together, I pray for God's strength so that we will be safe and secure without falling.

Now I feel that without God's guidance our lives feel quite fragile. So every night when I get ready to sleep, I offer gratitude to God: gratitude for today and for the salvation that Jesus gave through his sacrifice on the cross. It is that great love that gives strength to me and my family.

Prayer: *O God, the source of our life, guide us through this journey until we arrive at your house in heaven. In the name of the Lord, Jesus Christ, we pray. Amen.*

Thought for the day: When I ask, God can direct every step of my life.

Mee Kiem Oei (Central Java, Indonesia)

Present in our pain

Read Isaiah 38:9–20

Surely it was for my benefit that I suffered such anguish.

Isaiah 38:17 (NIV)

One summer evening, I flipped through my prayer journal filled with scribbled prayers, quotes and drawings. The journal was from a time I had struggled with anaemia, requiring multiple iron infusions. At the time, everything seemed uncertain. How many more infusions would I need? Would I ever experience healing?

As I reviewed my old journal, I saw the little ways God displayed loving care for me: a kind word from a nurse, the beauty of a sunset, a much-needed Bible verse.

Hezekiah also experienced an illness that brought him closer to God. After receiving the news that he would not recover from a serious illness, the king sought God's help through prayer. God answered by increasing Hezekiah's life by 15 years.

Although seasons of sickness are painful, they often push us to seek God's presence and help. We learn more about God's faithfulness as we trust God in the uncertainty of each day. If we are open to God's presence, we will also find that God is growing our faith. While we are in the midst of suffering, pain may affect our perspective. But when we take time to reflect, we will discover that God has been with us all along.

Prayer: *Dear Lord, help us to be aware of your loving presence when we are suffering in sickness or distress. Amen.*

Thought for the day: During times of affliction and suffering God never leaves me.

Sophia Bricker (North Carolina, USA)

God made us all different

Read Psalm 139:7–18

I praise you, for I am fearfully and wonderfully made. Wonderful are your works; that I know very well.

Psalm 139:14 (NRSV)

As I sat in my assigned plane seat, I took the opportunity to do a little people watching as the passengers began to flood onto the plane. I saw sad faces, happy faces, hurting faces, wrinkled faces, baby faces and even a set of faces that looked alike (twins, I presumed). I marvelled at the idea that no two people were the same, even the twins. It is amazing that God could create an entire human race and never repeat a single individual.

We are all different – in appearance, personalities, skills, abilities and attitudes. Psalm 139:14 talks about each of us being wonderfully made in the image of God. How marvellous to know that there is no one in the world like us! We are each perfectly made and one-of-a-kind.

When you have a little time on your hands, do some people watching. You will be amazed at the originality of what God has created. We each are loved and were created by God.

Prayer: *God, creator of all, we praise you for making us who we are. Help us to grow confidently into who you have made us to be. Use us today and help us represent you in all we do. Amen.*

Thought for the day: I am unique and loved by God.

Todd Diedrich (Wisconsin, USA)

 PRAYER FOCUS: TO APPRECIATE THE DIVERSITY IN CREATION

Life is uncertain

Read Job 1:13–22

You do not even know what tomorrow will bring. What is your life? For you are a mist that appears for a little while and then vanishes.

James 4:14 (NRSV)

Ten years ago, my brother-in-law died suddenly from a cardiac arrest. Within seconds, his two kids were left fatherless and their young mother became a widow. In the years since, Jesus has sustained the family and helped them through their grief. Though everything else in their lives changed, God did not.

Though in the blink of an eye we may lose everything, God never abandons us. Sometimes in moments of sorrow we can see God's love for us more clearly. In a day, Job lost his children and possessions. His life, once brimming with blessings, looked like a curse. But he remained faithful, saying, 'Naked I came from my mother's womb, and naked shall I return there; the Lord gave, and the Lord has taken away; blessed be the name of the Lord' (Job 1:21).

God desires such faith from us – that our devotion to God would remain strong even when we face struggles in life. May we hold on to God's promises, for they are true. We can take heart knowing that the God who helped Job in his deepest grief is with us too.

Prayer: *O God, help us to trust in you and you alone, no matter what we face. Amen.*

Thought for the day: Life is uncertain, but God never changes.

Amira Emmanuel (Khyber Pakhtunkhwa, Pakistan)

Hospitality and grace

Read James 2:1–13

Do not forget to show hospitality to strangers, for by so doing some people have shown hospitality to angels without knowing it.
Hebrews 13:2 (NIV)

When I was a child, a family trip to my godparents' house for the weekend was always a treat. My family lived in a crowded suburb, so the retreat to their very small town was an opportunity to explore freely and greet everyone openly.

The house itself was 100 years old, and the rooms seemed huge compared to our two-bedroom, post-war bungalow. The kitchen featured a large wooden table that managed to accommodate anyone who stopped by. Neighbours felt comfortable letting themselves in – sometimes cutting through the house instead of walking around the block – knowing the doors were never locked and coffee was always on. It was a home built upon hospitality and the grace of God.

Like our own homes, our houses of worship come in many styles and sizes – from grand cathedrals to one-room chapels. They are all created as a gathering place for those who love God, where we can enjoy the fellowship of the faithful, praise God, and gain strength and solace in times of trial. Jesus asked us to serve everyone with generous love, hope, forgiveness and grace as members of the family of God. When we do, our own faith is recharged, preparing us for sharing God's love when we leave.

Prayer: *Dear Lord, may we be filled with your presence every time we enter your house. Help us offer acceptance, hospitality and peace to all those who enter. Amen.*

Thought for the day: I will seek ways to live out the faith I practise in church.

Julia Clodius Cooke (Missouri, USA)

The crocus

Read Matthew 6:25–30

Anyone who needs wisdom should ask God, whose very nature is to give to everyone without a second thought, without keeping score. Wisdom will certainly be given to those who ask.

James 1:5 (CEB)

My life seemed to be in a slump, and I felt stuck. I went outside hoping a breath of fresh air would cheer me up. The snow had almost disappeared, and a cacophony of bird calls welcomed the spring. A soft south-westerly breeze greeted me, and the warmth of the sun on my face was delightful. A small patch of purple crocuses had bravely pushed through a clump of snow. I wondered how such tiny, delicate flowers had overcome the daunting obstacle of the frozen ground. It was a miracle – a hopeful sign of new life. I began to feel better as I reflected on the lilies of the field and the birds of the air that Jesus spoke about, marvelling at his providential care.

Not everything in life comes easily. We are faced with hard choices, challenges and obstacles at every turn. But when we walk with God we are not alone. God does not always remove our difficulties but gives us the wisdom to accept the struggle, the courage to meet the challenge and the strength to overcome. We need only ask.

Prayer: *Dear God, give us wisdom, courage and strength to face the obstacles that arise, trusting in you to walk with us through them all. Amen.*

Thought for the day: Where do I see signs of God's provision in my life?

Thomas Davis (Ontario, Canada)

The former things

Read Isaiah 43:18–21

'Forget the former things; do not dwell on the past. See, I am doing a new thing! Now it springs up; do you not perceive it? I am making a way in the wilderness and streams in the wasteland.'
Isaiah 43:18–19 (NIV)

I once went to an orchestra concert where the programme included *A German Requiem* by Johannes Brahms. The baritone solo at the beginning of the third movement was sung by a Grammy Award-winning opera singer who had been singing professionally for 26 years.

The soloist made his entrance at the right time but on the wrong note. The conductor calmly signalled a stop, then restarted the movement from the beginning. The second time the soloist's entrance was correct and the musicians successfully completed that segment of the requiem.

In the scripture above, God admonished the Israelites who were captive in Babylon to forget the past because God was going to do a new thing! When we make mistakes, God gives us the opportunity for a fresh start, just as it happened in the concert.

The season of Lent is a good time to surrender our former things to God. They might consist of a wrong action which hurt another person, a relationship that has deteriorated, a bad habit or a failure to act faithfully when the opportunity came to do good. We need only look to God for help in releasing that which dwells in our past, then moving on to a new and better future.

Prayer: *Gracious God, aid us in discerning what we need to release. Lead us to follow you in making all things new. Amen.*

Thought for the day: God invites me to release the past and embrace the present.

Carol Harbrecht Rice (Pennsylvania, USA)

 PRAYER FOCUS: FOR COURAGE TO LET GO OF THE PAST

Humble service

Read Romans 12:1–8

I thank Christ Jesus our Lord, who has given me strength, that he considered me trustworthy, appointing me to his service.

1 Timothy 1:12 (NIV)

In August 2021, our church started providing medical equipment like folding walkers, wheelchairs, toilet chairs and beds with handles to people in need. A committee was formed, and I was entrusted as the president. We helped many people.

While doing this work, I was inspired by the Bible stories that give insight about service. Jesus humbly served others many times. John 13:4–5 states: 'He got up from the meal, took off his outer clothing, and wrapped a towel round his waist. After that, he poured water into a basin and began to wash his disciples' feet.' Moreover, he served others when he healed people with leprosy, made the blind see and the lame walk, and healed people who were possessed. Scripture makes it clear that Jesus valued service and asked his followers to serve too. For example, Peter healed a man who could not walk (see Acts 3:1–10), and the story of the good Samaritan teaches the importance of service as well (see Luke 10:25–37).

We are called to serve with faith and joy. If we adopt an attitude of willingness to serve others, surely the Lord will work through us.

Prayer: *Merciful God, we pray that you will open our hearts and guide us to serve others joyfully. We thank you for hearing our prayers. Amen.*

Thought for the day: I live out God's call for my life when I serve others.

Jaiprakash D. Roy (Gujarat, India)

PRAYER FOCUS: FOR WILLINGNESS TO SERVE

Footsteps

Read Psalm 139:1–6

You created my inmost being; you knit me together in my mother's womb.

Psalm 139:13 (NIV)

My husband and I have three sons, and I noticed recently that I can easily identify each one by their footsteps on the stairs in our home. One goes quickly and jumps down the last few steps with a thud. Another has a lighter step, and the third has a steady, even gait. I cultivated this skill without even realising it!

I love and know my sons thoroughly. But as much as I know my sons, how much more does God – the one who knit me together in my mother's womb – know me! God knows my innermost thoughts. God knows what I will say, do or think before it happens. It's both comforting and unnerving to be so completely known. It's comforting because I am secure in God's love for me, but it's unnerving because I know that I am flawed. However, I think of my love for my sons. No matter their flaws or mistakes, I love them completely, and this reminds me of God's unconditional love for me. Even so, just as my children apologise and acknowledge their mistakes, I too must confess and repent of my sins.

It delighted me to discover that I have this special knowledge of my sons. I trust that God delights even more in knowing me.

Prayer: *Dear heavenly Father, thank you for creating us, knowing us and loving us completely. May our footsteps always follow yours. In Jesus' name. Amen.*

Thought for the day: I am a beloved child of God.

Amy Oyler (Georgia, USA)

An unexpected guide

Read Deuteronomy 34:9–12

As iron sharpens iron, so one person sharpens another.

Proverbs 27:17 (NIV)

I have spent more than 30 years teaching children with behavioural disorders. But I think back to a time when I considered leaving the education field. Thankfully, God sent me a mentor and brother in Christ to help guide me during this uncertain time. Sonny was our school's custodian, and one day he gave me a copy of *The Upper Room*. Afterward, Sonny would drop by my room each day and we would discuss the readings together.

I am grateful to God for sending Sonny as a mentor. I have continued a fulfilling career and now work with juveniles who were incarcerated. In addition, I've been given an opportunity to be a mentor to many co-workers. I give them *The Upper Room* just as Sonny did for me. Today, Sonny delivers copies of each issue to me so that I can give a copy to those I mentor.

God is unfailing when we need someone to help direct our path. In scripture God provided Joshua instruction through Moses to lead Israel to the promised land (Deuteronomy 34:9). Elijah inspired Elisha, who assumed Elijah's ministry (1 Kings 19:16). In what we might see as an impossible challenge, God is at work providing the direction we need to serve others.

Prayer: *Dear God, guide our steps and direct our paths. Show us opportunities to grow and to be of service to you in unexpected ways. Amen.*

Thought for the day: For whom is God calling me to be a mentor?

Mark Hailey (South Carolina, USA)

PRAYER FOCUS: YOUNG PERSONS WHO NEED GUIDANCE

A new spirit

Read Psalm 51:10–12

Create in me a clean heart, O God, and put a new and right spirit within me.

Psalm 51:10 (NRSV)

During Lent, many Christians embark on a journey of spiritual growth and reflection, echoing Jesus Christ's 40 days in the wilderness. This sacred time invites us to deepen our relationship with God and others and prepares our hearts to remember Christ's passion, death and resurrection.

The story of Jesus' temptation in the wilderness emphasises the importance of self-control and relying on God's strength during tough times (see Matthew 4:1–11). In Matthew 6:16–18, Jesus teaches that fasting should be done humbly and without seeking praise from others. This reminds us that Lenten practices are not just outward acts but expressions of inner devotion and repentance. Lent also encourages reflection on Jesus' teachings about love for God and neighbour. Lent is an opportunity to examine our lives in light of Jesus' teachings and to seek forgiveness and renewal.

Lent is a path towards spiritual growth and transformation and a deeper understanding of God's love and grace. Through prayer, fasting and acts of kindness, we can draw closer to God, allowing the Spirit to shape us into vessels of God's love.

Prayer: *Dear God, guide us in our spiritual journey to become more like you and help us to maintain our focus on you. In Jesus' name we pray. Amen.*

Thought for the day: Lenten practices prepare my heart and spirit to embrace the joy of Easter.

Penny Wachira (Nairobi, Kenya)

God's patchwork quilt

Read Isaiah 55:8–13

'So is my word that goes out from my mouth: it will not return to me empty.'

Isaiah 55:11 (NIV)

I love how in patchwork, one can take scraps of cloth, material that often would otherwise be discarded, and stitch them together to make a large, beautiful, colourful quilt. It is a wonderful metaphor for how God works.

I recently read a good example of this in the story of a mission worker in South America. He had commissioned a local carpenter to do a job, paying for the materials upfront, and during one of his visits he had also given the man a Bible. Unfortunately, the mission worker eventually learned that the carpenter had spent all the money on drink, and the work he had paid for never materialised. It felt like a waste of time, money and effort.

Ten years later, the mission worker was approached by a young man who asked, 'Remember me?' He was one of the carpenter's children. While the carpenter had not read the Bible he'd been gifted, the children had. As a result, the young man had become a mission worker himself, and all his siblings were also Christians! The mission worker concluded: 'God can pick up all the scraps you thought had gone to waste, and make something beautiful out of them in the end.'

As Isaiah prophesied all those years ago, God's word never gets wasted. The same is true today: never lose heart about prayers, gifts, words and actions that seemingly go unnoticed. God recycles everything. We are all part of God's patchwork quilt!

Prayer: *Dear Lord, thank you, that you bless every faithful step we take, no matter how small. Amen.*

Thought for the day: God chooses the 'things that are not – to nullify the things that are' (see 1 Corinthians 1:28).

Iris Lloyd (England, United Kingdom)

God's word

Read 1 John 5:13–15

If we know that [God] listens to whatever we ask, we know that we have received what we asked from him.

1 John 5:15 (CEB)

Doña Bertitha had already lost several children. Now she looked at her tiny infant daughter – born at six months gestation, anaemic, suffering from a heart condition, and having already received a blood transfusion. Doctors told Bertitha that if her daughter survived, she would have serious health challenges. But Bertitha's father-in-law Don Rafael shared the word of God with her and said: 'Believe, and it shall be done!' Holding hands, they prayed on their knees. Bertitha held fast to the promise of a miracle. Day by day that miracle began to unfold, much to the surprise of the medical staff.

This is my life story. I was that child. I grew up and became a faithful follower of Christ. Later, I cared for my parents and my own children, and now I rejoice at seeing my grandchildren thrive. Throughout my life I have experienced many miracles and continue to believe in God's word. Imagine the possibilities if we all opened our hearts and minds to God's promises and miracles!

Prayer: *Thank you, loving God, for all the unexpected gifts you give us. Strengthen us through your word, and inspire us with your promises. Amen.*

Thought for the day: God can work miracles.

Rebeca Castellanos Barajas (Mexico City, Mexico)

Doubly blessed

Read 1 Corinthians 12:12–14, 26–27

If one part suffers, every part suffers with it; if one part is honoured, every part rejoices with it. Now you are the body of Christ, and each one of you is a part of it.

1 Corinthians 12:26–27 (NIV)

Last week our church observed Communion. Because of health issues, I was unable to go forward to receive the sacrament. One of the ushers noticed my problem and asked if I would like for the servers to bring the bread and cup to me, but I was reluctant. However, when they brought the elements to a woman in the row behind me, my friend motioned for them to serve me as well. I was humbled by this unexpected hospitality.

The server holding the loaf bent over and softly said, 'The body of Christ broken for you', as she placed a small piece of bread in my palm. Her companion leaned over and held the cup out to me so I could dip the bread in it. In a soft voice he said, 'The blood of Christ shed for you.'

I had heard both these phrases spoken dozens of times before, but this time they reached through all my mental clutter and touched me on a deeply personal level. Two of God's servants answered the call of someone in need without fanfare or hesitation. So I was doubly blessed – by the sacrament itself and by their loving outreach to me. In that moment they exemplified what it means to be part of the body of Christ.

Prayer: *Dear Lord, guide us in fulfilling our role as a part of your church. Help us to grow in our strength and understanding of your will for the world you created. Amen.*

Thought for the day: Each of us has our role to play as part of the body of Christ.

Carol P. Nyborg (North Carolina, USA)

PRAYER FOCUS: SOMEONE WHO HAS NOTICED MY NEEDS

All things for our good

Read Genesis 45:1–8

We know that in all things God works for the good of those who love him, who have been called according to his purpose.
Romans 8:28 (NIV)

In my last year of university studies, my parents were not able to afford my tuition. I felt God had let me down, especially because I was committed to ministry.

During the next year and a half, I wrote my first book, joined a school outreach ministry at my church and made many helpful relationships. Then, thankfully, with God's provision, I was able to complete my studies.

The apostle Paul reminds us to trust God's process and presence regardless of our circumstances. Even when it seems as if God is silent and distant, we know God is weaving our sufferings into a testimony and forming compassion in us for those who suffer. I recall the story of Joseph. His brothers hated him and sold him into slavery in Egypt where he became a servant, was falsely accused and thrown into prison. After some years, when Joseph met his brothers again, rather than seek revenge, Joseph chose to save their lives (see Genesis 45:7).

When we face unexpected and unpleasant situations, we may be tempted to doubt God, be anxious or seek solutions that are not rooted in faith. We may not understand why we're going through a tough season, but God knows and cares about every detail of our lives.

Prayer: *Heavenly Father, forgive us for doubting you. Thank you for working all things for our good. Amen.*

Thought for the day: Every day I will wait on the Lord.

Hirwa G. Israel (Kampala, Uganda)

Ignoring our blessings

Read Psalm 100

Throw all your anxiety onto [God], because he cares about you.
1 Peter 5:7 (CEB)

This morning I watched in amusement as our bulldog, Archie, puzzled over a toy that had rolled under a footstool. He peered beneath the footstool and pawed repeatedly at the red ball, which remained just beyond his reach. Finally he sat down in frustration, looked at me and whined plaintively. I laughed aloud and moved the stool while Archie happily pounced on the ball and trotted off with it.

Archie has many toys, but watching him ignore all the others while he fixated on the one toy he could not have made me think. We humans can get trapped by that same mindset. We can become so intent on the one thing we can't, don't or shouldn't have that we ignore the many blessings in our lives.

Recently I was so overwhelmed with solving a problem (which was not my responsibility) that I lost all pleasure in life. Thankfully, God patiently showed me how I was allowing the problem to keep me from enjoying the beautiful life God has given me. Now, though it is still unsolved, I give the problem to God who alone has the ability to take care of it. And I focus my energy on appreciating all that God has done for me in other areas.

Prayer: *Patient and loving God, even though it's hard sometimes, help us to trust you to resolve the overwhelming issues we face. Keep us ever mindful of all we have to be grateful for. Amen.*

Thought for the day: Even in times of challenge, I have much to thank God for.

DeVonna R. Allison (Florida, USA)

Play our part

Read Acts 2:42–47

All the believers were together and had everything in common.
Acts 2:44 (NIV)

While my husband and I were travelling for our anniversary, we attended a bluegrass jam of about 30 musicians. As the evening began, it was explained that each musician would get to lead a song. They would take turns naming a tune, the key it was to be played in, and the order in which the parts of the song were to be played.

Throughout the night, as each musician laid out the plan for their song, others joined in and built it up, harmonising and supporting the performance of the leader. Watching them work together by listening carefully to one another with no written music or lyrics to guide them was beautiful and inspiring. Even the strongest musicians made space for others.

The music was a wonderful gift that night, but even more so was the vision of this community that was so clearly built on love and supportiveness. It reminded me of what the disciples must have been trying to create in the early church: a community where everyone shared what they had and everyone benefited in the sharing. I left that night with a template of what such a community might look like and a prayer in my heart that we will all play our part in making it a reality.

Prayer: *Dear God, widen our hearts to envision all of humanity as our family and community. Help us to care for our neighbours and lift them up in word and deed. Amen.*

Thought for the day: Today I will find a way to lift up others.

Dawn M. Adams (New Hampshire, USA)

God sees and hears us

God heard their groaning, and God remembered his covenant with Abraham, Isaac, and Jacob. God looked upon the Israelites, and God took notice of them.
Exodus 2:24–25 (NRSV)

A while ago, I was talking to a relative, but I wasn't sure that she was paying attention to me. When I asked her if she was, she said, 'I am seeing and hearing you.' Sometimes we might wonder if God is paying attention to us, but scripture assures us that God sees and hears us constantly.

When the people of Israel found themselves living a hard reality in Egypt, the Bible says that God heard their groaning and remembered his covenant with Abraham, Isaac and Jacob, and that God looked upon the children of Israel and took notice of them. In this story, God not only sees and hears the Israelites, but God demonstrates the fundamental qualities of faithfulness and mercy as well.

As God's people were suffering the ravages of slavery in Egypt, it would have been easy for them to think that God had forgotten them. Exodus 2:23 says, 'The Israelites groaned under their slavery and cried out.' Deprived of their freedom and basic human rights, their suffering was great. Though many of us cannot personally relate to the Israelites' experience of slavery, today, people in parts of the world still live in situations of immense oppression where they are denied their most fundamental freedoms.

We currently find ourselves in a time when the social, political, economic and environmental landscapes are unclear. What's more, it seems that there is an increasing indifference towards loving God and our neighbour – two ideas that are at the foundation of our faith. I think this leads to an even greater uncertainty about what the future holds and paints a discouraging picture of spiritual decline.

Like the people of Israel, we might start to think that God has forgotten us. But in turbulent times, we can remind ourselves that our cry goes out to God, and God hears us. God remembers God's covenant with and love for us. God not only hears us but, as scripture says, *God takes notice of us*.

What does this recognition of us mean? It means that the God who created us knows who we are, down to the most intimate fibre of our being. God knows our circumstances, our reality, our fears and our conflicts. God hears our moans and our cries. God is faithful to us and does not abandon us.

Sometimes I hear expressions of resignation from people who think that our world is going from bad to worse. Such a belief saddens me. Instead, I like to imagine that we are floating in an ark over seas of turbulence and suffering but still being cared for by our Lord. I have faith that one day the waters will recede, and we will be able to contemplate the light of a new day full of hope.

In this new year, may we look towards the future with hope and the certainty that our God sees us, listens to us and recognises our suffering. May we also see and hear the cries of our neighbours and do what we can to help them. God walks with us and can lead us out of the most difficult of circumstances.

QUESTIONS FOR REFLECTION

1. When have you felt that God does not see you or hear you? What was that experience like? When have you felt that God does see you and hear you? What did this teach you about God's presence?
2. What does the message 'God looked upon the Israelites, and God took notice of them' mean to you? In what ways does it encourage you and give you hope?
3. How can we see and listen more attentively to those around us? What spiritual practices help remind us that God will never abandon us?

Jorge L. Berríos, editor of El Aposento Alto, The Upper Room – Spanish-language edition

Spring is on the way

Read Psalm 139:1–12

Even the darkness will not be dark to you; the night will shine like the day, for darkness is as light to you.

Psalm 139:12 (NIV)

I live in the far north, and as winter sets in, the nights become long and all of creation seems to lie dormant. People often feel downcast. You read it in their faces. You see it in the way they brace against the wind and pass by looking at the ground, their focus only on reaching their destination.

Feeling the onslaught of this weariness, I decided to go forward for prayer one Sunday morning. The pastor prayed for me and then paused. I still remember what he said next: 'Spring is on the way!' He was right. Skies eventually became blue and days got longer. People started to smile and stopped to talk in the streets.

It can be like that in our spiritual lives as well. Jesus never said the narrow way would be easy. On the contrary. He told us to expect trouble and warned us that the way ahead would be demanding. But Jesus promised that he would be with us all the way. What a comfort it is to know that we are not expected to walk this path alone.

And that is how we find joy even when it is still winter. Through faith we hold on to the assurance that the Lord is with us, and spring is on the way.

Prayer: *Dear God, help us to keep our eyes on you, knowing that you are with us even when the night is long. Amen.*

Thought for the day: 'For, lo, the winter is past, the rain is over and gone' (Song of Songs 2:11, KJV).

Carol Westerlund (Uusimaa, Finland)

Called to serve

Read Jeremiah 29:11–12

I heard the voice of the Lord saying, 'Whom shall I send? And who will go for us?' And I said, 'Here am I. Send me!'
Isaiah 6:8 (NIV)

When I was just out of college, my first job was working at a psychiatric hospital as a healthcare technician, helping children and adolescents. In school, I had taken an interests inventory, and my two highest scoring areas were counselling and pastoral ministry. God seemed to be calling me, but I wasn't sure in what direction. As I prayed for guidance, the words of Isaiah 6:8 came to mind: 'Here am I. Send me!'

My experience at the hospital helped me decide to attend graduate school and pursue a career in counselling. I felt God calling me to support young people and their families, bringing them encouragement and hope. God had sent important people to me in my young life when I needed help, and I felt it was time to pay that forward.

Now that I am retired, I give thanks to God for my career in counselling as well as the experiences my family and I have had serving in church over the years. My wife and I are blessed to serve as lay people in our congregation. Sometimes I wonder how my life might have been different if I had become a pastor. However, I believe as Christians we're able to minister to others, even if we're not ordained pastors in a church. God has a plan for each one of us!

Prayer: *Father God, thank you for guiding us as we show your love to others. Help us to trust in your plans for us. Amen.*

Thought for the day: In what ways is God calling me to minister to others today?

Robert Brooks (North Carolina, USA)

Scanning my life

Read 2 Timothy 3:10–17

Every scripture is inspired by God and is useful for teaching, for showing mistakes, for correcting, and for training character, so that the person who belongs to God can be equipped to do everything that is good.

2 Timothy 3:16–17 (CEB)

A few years ago, a technician instructed me to lie on my back for a scan to evaluate my bone density. When I did, I felt as if my back were crooked. I adjusted my position until I felt comfortable and like my back was straight.

Following the test, the technician showed me the scan; I was surprised to see that my upper back was leaning to the right. My 'straight' back was not straight at all. My perception of comfort and alignment was out of sync with the reality revealed by the scan.

This is also an easy mistake for me to make in my spiritual life. What I think is comfortable and right with respect to God's plan and purpose may actually be misaligned. I have realised that it is important to check my thoughts and actions against the truth of God's word regularly. Paul's words in 2 Timothy 3:14–15 describe practical tools for examining and correcting our ways by studying the godly example of others and the words of scripture. These help me scan my life so I can stay correctly aligned in my faith.

Prayer: *Dear God, as we seek your plan and purpose for our lives, keep us from leaning on our own counsel. May we stay on the straight path of your ways. Amen.*

Thought for the day: How is my life aligned with God's ways?

Diane Boleyn (Iowa, USA)

PRAYER FOCUS: THOSE HAVING MEDICAL TESTS

Compassion

Read Matthew 14:12–21

When Jesus landed and saw a large crowd, he had compassion on them and healed those who were ill.

Matthew 14:14 (NIV)

When reading the familiar story of Jesus feeding the 5,000, we may be in such a hurry to take notice of Jesus' miracle that we miss an important detail: Jesus had compassion *for* others at a time when he needed compassion *from* others. Jesus had decided to spend time with his disciples away from the crowd after he learned that John the Baptist had been beheaded. But the crowd followed Jesus and was waiting for him when he stepped out of the boat. If I had been in Jesus' shoes, I might have complained about the crowd or angrily demanded that they leave. But instead, 'when Jesus landed and saw a large crowd, he had compassion on them'.

Jesus had compassion on the crowd even though he had just learned about his cousin's death and was hoping to spend some quiet time alone. But Jesus showed us that we can offer compassion in all circumstances. Even when we are going through troubles of our own, may we imitate our Lord's example and have compassion on others.

Prayer: *God of compassion, in our world filled with people who are hurting and in need, help us always to imitate our compassionate Lord. In Jesus' name we pray. Amen.*

Thought for the day: I imitate Christ when I show compassion.

Jeremy K. Mullen (Pennsylvania, USA)

 PRAYER FOCUS: TO SHOW COMPASSION EVEN WHEN IT IS DIFFICULT

Beside quiet waters

Read Psalm 23

He makes me lie down in green pastures, he leads me beside quiet waters.

Psalm 23:2 (NIV)

I like to be busy. If a friend is looking for a tennis or running buddy, I usually say yes. I raise my hand when my church needs volunteers. I try to meet the needs I see in my community.

I love my full, vibrant life, but sometimes it becomes too much. When I pile on too many obligations, I become stressed and irritable. I know I need to rest, but it can be hard to resist the temptation of constant activity because then I feel like I'm letting people down.

In those times, my Saviour reminds me how important rest is for my soul. He leads me into rhythms of sabbath and restoration. I don't always know what I need, but thankfully God does. If we take time each day to sit and savour God's word and love, our priorities will begin to look more like God's.

When I am tempted to fill every moment with activity, the Lord reminds me of the importance of lying down in green pastures and the simple joy of strolling beside quiet waters. When I spend time with Jesus in silence, I'm not missing out on anything.

Prayer: *Dear God, help us take time to rest. Revive and restore us so we can serve our families, churches and communities from a place of wholeness and peace. Amen.*

Thought for the day: I will find time today to rest in the presence of my Saviour.

Jillian Bell (Ontario, Canada)

The gift of faith

Read Isaiah 41:8–10

'I am with you always, to the very end of the age.'
Matthew 28:20 (NIV)

One day when I was six years old, my mum said she had something to tell me. Wringing her hands, she said, 'Delsie, I want you to know that God, Jesus and the Holy Spirit will always take care of you and our family. No matter what.' As I listened, I didn't really know what she meant. Tears flowed down her pale cheeks, and I wondered what was wrong. What was she trying to tell me?

A few weeks later, Mum was admitted to a psychiatric hospital where she stayed for two years. As time dragged on, there wasn't a day that I didn't cry for her. However, I also remembered what she had told me. Missing her made me physically ache, but her words continued to echo in my heart and mind. Somehow I knew I was not alone.

The faith-filled words she spoke to me before going to the hospital have been a lifelong gift to me. They have helped me to grow strong in my faith over time. When Mum finally returned home, she had been through a lot; but we were jubilant to have her back with us. This childhood experience taught me to place my trust and hope in God, Jesus and the Holy Spirit.

Prayer: *Triune God, thank you for the gift of faith and for all the blessings you have given us. Amen.*

Thought for the day: My faith grows when I put my trust and hope in God.

Adele M. Gill (Maryland, USA)

Daily routine

Read Acts 18:18–23

After spending some time in Antioch, Paul set out from there and travelled from place to place throughout the region of Galatia and Phrygia, strengthening all the disciples.
Acts 18:23 (NIV)

A year ago I experienced a debilitating stroke that sent me to the hospital for 16 days. This past year has been challenging, but I was fortunate not to lose the use of my right side. However, the stroke did severely weaken that side. I spent nearly two hours every weekday exercising to strengthen it. Some days the monotony of exercise was boring, but everyone told me that exercising was necessary to continue my recovery.

I was reading the above passage from Acts 18 and realised that Paul must have had times where his daily work felt monotonous. While Paul had some amazing and eventful times, those moments were built upon the routine portions of his life that were vital for his ministry.

After reading these verses, I was more motivated while doing my daily exercises. Seeing steady progress in my recovery, I realised that while God sometimes heals through miracles, more often God heals us through our daily routines. I give thanks that God gives us the strength and wisdom to carry them out.

Prayer: *Father God, we pray that you will enable us to carry on in doing your will, even when our daily work feels monotonous. Amen.*

Thought for the day: My daily routine can be a source of spiritual growth.

Steven Thompson (Iowa, USA)

The path to salvation

Read Hebrews 12:1–13

The Lord is my shepherd. I lack nothing.

Psalm 23:1 (CEB)

My late grandmother endured a difficult life. She married a man who never truly learned how to love. Yet she devoted her life to supporting her family and lived solely for their needs. There were many times when she was abandoned by her husband and needed someone by her side, but no one – not even her children – was there.

Still she persevered in faith. In times of hardship she prayed to God, and in times of blessing she gave thanks for the daily bread God provided. She never gave up on her faith, and in the end, her perseverance bore fruit: her husband changed and one of her children became a pastor. Today, her descendants number over 30, and we all know God.

When she finally lay at rest in her coffin, a white cloth inscribed with the words The Lord Was My Salvation was draped over her. She triumphed over every hardship, faithfully walking the path to salvation, and at last she was able to see God.

My grandmother's faith has inspired my own. May all the people around the world persevere in faith to the end and, like my grandmother, meet God at the finish line.

Prayer: *Faithful God, give us the strength and ability to endure and overcome our challenges as we walk the path of faith. Amen.*

Thought for the day: God helps me persevere in faith to the end.

Binnah Kim (South Korea)

A knock at the door

Read Revelation 3:20–22

Listen! I am standing at the door, knocking; if you hear my voice and open the door, I will come in and eat with you, and you with me.
Revelation 3:20 (NRSV)

I was blessed with a happy childhood surrounded by the love of my parents, siblings and extended family. I can recall few moments of disappointment in my early life, but one of those were times when we went to visit my grandparents only to discover that they were out. This was before everyone had landline phones (let alone mobiles), so we couldn't let them know in advance that we were coming. We would knock at the door in anticipation of their loving welcome and hospitality, including our favourite food, only to be disappointed when the door did not open.

I started to wonder if God experienced disappointment, too. In Revelation, John has a vision of Jesus saying that he knocks at the door of our hearts, eagerly wanting us to invite him in and eat with us. I wonder how many times God has knocked on the door of my heart before I opened it, and how God might have felt before an unopened door. I guess disappointed and sad.

Fortunately, we have a God whose love never wavers. God does not break down the door, but God does persist in knocking. Each day we should be listening for that knock, ready to answer God's call.

Prayer: *Dear God, thank you that you eagerly desire to make your home in our hearts through your Holy Spirit. Amen.*

Thought for the day: I will open the door to Jesus today.

Faith Ford (England, United Kingdom)

PRAYER FOCUS: GRANDPARENTS

Nowhere to sit

Read 1 John 4:7–12

'The King will reply, "Truly I tell you, whatever you did for one of the least of these brothers and sisters of mine, you did for me."'
Matthew 25:40 (NIV)

When I started high school, I was very shy and had no friends at school. When I entered the cafeteria for lunch and looked for a place to sit, it seemed that everyone was already sitting with their friends – talking, laughing and enjoying their food.

When two students welcomed me to sit with them, it was such a relief not to have to sit alone. Myra and Terri, who were both Christians, showed me kindness and helped make the school day much better for me. I felt included and wanted, and I will never forget the way they showed God's love to me.

People today, especially young people, face similar situations. When we see someone sitting alone, we can go and be a friend, welcoming them and sharing God's love and inclusion. Everything we do has consequences, and our compassionate actions can change lives for the good.

Prayer: *Dear Father, help us to be a beacon of hope to others, welcoming them as you welcome us. We pray the prayer your Son taught us, 'Our Father in heaven, hallowed be your name, your kingdom come, your will be done, on earth as it is in heaven. Give us today our daily bread. And forgive us our debts, as we also have forgiven our debtors. And lead us not into temptation, but deliver us from the evil one' (Matthew 6:9–13, NIV). Amen.*

Thought for the day: I will welcome and love others as God welcomes me.

Vicki Keith (Virginia, USA)

 PRAYER FOCUS: THOSE WHO FEEL EXCLUDED AND ALONE

Diving deeper

Read Psalm 8

When I consider your heavens, the work of your fingers, the moon and the stars, which you have set in place, what is mankind that you are mindful of them, human beings that you care for them?

Psalm 8:3–4 (NIV)

One morning I went for my usual swim in a clear pool in the ocean. As I was snorkelling, I suddenly found myself among a large school of tiny fish. Soon I noticed they were forming a circle around me. What a joyous experience, being in the centre of a perfect circle of hundreds or maybe thousands of little fish! I wanted to share this joy with someone else and surfaced to see if anyone else noticed this amazing sight, but everyone was just having fun floating, enjoying a wonderful morning in the sea.

I couldn't help thinking that – just as my goggles enable me to see below the surface and experience the beauty of God's creation – a relationship with Christ allows me to experience the overwhelming joy of life lived at a deeper spiritual level. Many people seem happy swimming on the surface of life, not realising that they are missing out on the very best life has to offer: a personal relationship with our creator. When I put on the goggles of faith and dive into the ocean of God's word, the Holy Spirit reveals a whole new world to me, and I experience the joy of realising who I am in Christ!

Prayer: *Loving God, give us a desire to seek you. Bring us ever closer to you as we study your word and do your will. Amen.*

Thought for the day: Scripture gives me a deeper connection to God.

Estelle Hopkins (Paphos, Cyprus)

A calf's cry

Read Isaiah 30:19–22

In their hearts humans plan their course, but the Lord establishes their steps.

Proverbs 16:9 (NIV)

It was mid-morning and I was sitting on our porch, looking out at the pasture. As the sun rose higher and higher, the herd of cattle that had grazed overnight in the open grassland moved to the cool shade offered by a grove of large oak and pecan trees.

I noticed a small, solitary calf haltingly approach the cows now resting in the grove. It surveyed the herd and let out a mournful wail, as if saying, 'Mother, I am lost and alone. I need your help.' It took two plaintive calls, but the calf's mother recognised its cries and responded with her own. I imagined she was saying, 'Here I am, child.' The calf heard its mother's call, and they were soon reunited.

That scene reminded me that when we feel lost or need help, we can always seek God for assurance and direction. Life can be confusing, and it can be difficult to know the next step to take or how to solve a problem. Like the small calf, we need to call out to our loving provider and seek guidance. We must admit our need and ask for direction. And when we do so, we can be assured that God, our comforter, hears us and will provide guidance.

Prayer: *God of clarity, when we are lost, lead us to call out for your direction, and give us patience as we await your response. Amen.*

Thought for the day: I will pay close attention to how God is responding to me and trust God's leading.

John Alter (Florida, USA)

Transitions

Read Psalm 27

Wait for the Lord; be strong and take heart and wait for the Lord.
Psalm 27:14 (NIV)

When my normally prolific irises didn't bloom, I consulted a friend who is an accomplished gardener. She advised me to move them to an area with more sunlight. I did so, but alas, only one of the dozen plants flowered the following spring. I learned that many plants don't bloom the year after they are transplanted. It takes them a while to adjust to their new surroundings. The next year they produced 52 flowers! It was worth the wait.

Transitions can be hard for people too. After earning a degree in education, I got a job teaching history at a junior high school. The first year was unbelievably challenging, and I was tempted to quit. But with no other job options, I went back for a second year. As I grew accustomed to my surroundings, I began to flourish and became an effective teacher.

Three years later, I took a job with a prison ministry that included a considerable amount of teaching. I might have felt unqualified had I not persevered in my earlier job. Now I can see that God graciously walked with me during that first year of teaching – a difficult time that nonetheless prepared me for what was to come. Since then I have faced other transitions with more confidence, knowing God can use all those changes to produce fruit in me.

Prayer: *Gracious Father, thank you for transforming us when we are transplanted so that we can bloom even more abundantly. In Jesus' name. Amen.*

Thought for the day: Challenging times can be the times of greatest growth.

Lisa Stackpole (Wisconsin, USA)

PRAYER FOCUS: SOMEONE TRANSITIONING TO A NEW JOB

A powerful vision

Read Acts 2:42–47

Where there is no vision, the people perish: but he that keepeth the law, happy is he.

Proverbs 29:18 (KJV)

In our small rural community, two churches were struggling with declining attendance and aging congregations. Rather than succumb to despair, the leaders of the churches united and crafted a shared vision to uplift Christ in our community.

Our church leaders understood the power of a shared vision. Over the next five years, through diligent prayer, meticulous planning and unwavering perseverance, we worked to bring their vision to fruition. The journey was riddled with challenges and demanded sacrifices from both congregations. However, our faith and commitment to a unified vision propelled us forward.

Today, our merged church is thriving. Our new, shared building serves as a place of worship and a hub for outreach ministries. We host sports programmes, support groups, weddings and wakes, fostering a tighter bond within our community during times of both joy and sorrow.

Throughout this transformative journey, we've witnessed Proverbs 29:18 in action. By adhering to our vision and following God's guidance, we've built a church that is flourishing as a beacon of hope and support for our community.

Prayer: *Dear Lord, help us to seek your guidance and remain united in purpose so that we may thrive and serve our communities well. Amen.*

Thought for the day: I can build up my community by following God's guidance.

Gerry Dale Stover (West Virginia, USA)

Refraining from judgement

Read Job 4:1–6

'Now trouble comes to you, and you are discouraged; it strikes you, and you are dismayed.'

Job 4:5 (NIV)

After a series of failed jobs and a financial crisis, I was filled with anxiety. For over 10 years, I had prayed for a stable job. Every job I started seemed to be from the Lord, yet I ended up either losing or giving each one up because I was unable to cope with the pressure.

I could not understand God's plan and started expressing my pain openly. But as a believer actively involved in ministry, I was met with sharp criticism. Some people interpreted my situation as God's judgement and felt that my anxiety undermined my witness to others. However, some were compassionate and offered prayer, moral support and financial aid.

During this difficult season, the book of Job brought me great comfort, affirming my faith in God in the midst of the difficulties I was experiencing. Unlike Job's friends, who offered lofty insights and judgemental advice, God was pleased with Job – despite his bitter complaints (see Job 42:7–15). This experience taught me a fundamental lesson about empathy and strengthened my resolve to trust in God's provision. Only God can make an accurate assessment of one's faith. Our duty is to love and show compassion to those in pain.

Prayer: *Dear God, help us to refrain from making quick judgements. Instead, help us to be more empathetic and loving towards those in pain. Amen.*

Thought for the day: Today I will offer compassion to those who are hurting.

Elina Yeptho (Nagaland, India)

Wherever we are

Read Jeremiah 29:4–7

'For I know the plans I have for you,' declares the Lord, 'plans to prosper you and not to harm you, plans to give you hope and a future.'
Jeremiah 29:11 (NIV)

I was riding my electric bicycle along a rural road and stopped on a bridge to admire the scenic views. There was a small river below and mountains all around. In the middle of the stream was a large boulder – its top just inches above the fast-moving water. I was surprised to see a leafy sapling growing from the rock. It looked to be about three feet tall and in good health. From my vantage point above, I could detect no other growth on the rock. Whether the seed was blown there by the wind or dropped by a bird, the young tree had somehow found a foothold and was flourishing.

I thought of today's reading in Jeremiah. It encourages us to embrace our current circumstances – to survive and even thrive – knowing that God has a plan for our lives and for how we can be of service to others.

Wherever we find ourselves in life, there are many ways we can bless others as we accept God's blessings for us. We can reflect Christ and offer Christian witness in our communities through our acts of forgiveness and love.

Prayer: *Gracious God, show us opportunities to bless others wherever we are. Amen.*

Thought for the day: God can use me to make a difference wherever I am.

Robert E. Boertien (Oregon, USA)

God's love

Read 1 Samuel 16:1–13

'The Lord does not look at the things people look at. People look at the outward appearance, but the Lord looks at the heart.'

1 Samuel 16:7 (NIV)

I have moles, warts, red spots, dark spots, cysts, skin tags and more, and I sometimes feel deep shame that I have these unwanted marks. Over the years I have seen dermatologists to have many of these blemishes removed.

On a recent visit, one of my doctors noted how soft my skin was and said I did a great job moisturising. Another said I had excellent tone in my arm muscles and must be exercising regularly. I appreciated that they were able to see past things that bother me so much and focus on the positive and the effort I put into caring for my body.

But isn't this exactly what God does in our lives? God looks past our blemishes and sees the good – always encouraging us to do our best and then supporting us to move forward. In fact, in 1 Samuel 16:7, Samuel is instructed not to consider the outward appearance of a person but to look at the heart of a person like God does.

I'm thankful I can serve the Lord no matter my outer appearance. I'm even more thankful that God loves and accepts every one of us just the way we are – sometimes warts and all!

Prayer: *Dear Lord, thank you for looking past our flaws and examining our hearts to see the good within us. Amen.*

Thought for the day: God loves me just the way I am.

Jeannie Pagni Smith (Nevada, USA)

PRAYER FOCUS: TO ACCEPT MYSELF AS I AM

Gardening with God

Read Galatians 5:16–26

Live by the Spirit, and you will not gratify the desires of the flesh. For the flesh desires what is contrary to the Spirit, and the Spirit what is contrary to the flesh. They are in conflict with each other, so that you are not to do whatever you want.

Galatians 5:16–17 (NIV)

This year I have a community garden plot where I can grow vegetables. A few months after planting the seedlings and seeds, I am still enjoying the garden. But I had forgotten just how persistent and stubborn weeds are.

Week after week, it feels like I am pulling the same weeds from the same spots! It is amazing to me how quickly the weeds grow and how fast they can get out of hand if I miss a week of weeding. While the vegetables I have planted are steadily getting stronger and healthier, I am struck by the sheer determination of the weeds to grow despite repeatedly being ripped out.

How often do our lives parallel this scenario? God's Spirit grows the fruit of 'love, joy, peace, forbearance, kindness, goodness, faithfulness, gentleness and self-control' in us (see Galatians 5:22–23). But there are weeds in our lives too: envy, cruel responses, anger, unforgiveness or self-defeat. These things can be difficult to remove, but we must deal with them at the root. The good news is that we aren't tackling the weeds alone. We have a faithful, compassionate gardener who works in us and with us, helping us uproot the weeds and nurturing the fruit in us.

Prayer: *Gracious God, thank you for the work of transformation you are doing in us. Amen.*

Thought for the day: It is not my own will, but God's work in me, that transforms me.

Megan P. (Ontario, Canada)

A lesson in humility

Read John 13:1–17

God opposes the proud but shows favour to the humble.
James 4:6 (NIV)

The story of the Lord's supper is told in all four gospels. However, Luke's gospel includes a passage that is not mentioned in the other three.

Luke writes that the disciples were arguing about which of them would be considered the greatest. I find it interesting that their prideful boasting occurred while Jesus was doing the exact opposite. In a remarkable act of humility, he stunned his disciples by removing his outer garment and washing their feet. Humility was despised in the ancient world as a sign of weakness, yet Jesus willingly did a task usually done by the lowest of servants. Even though he was just hours from his crucifixion, Jesus wanted to make sure his followers learned an important lesson about serving others.

I can relate to the story because I've certainly struggled with pride at times. I think many of us have, since western culture often encourages us to focus on ourselves. But when we look to the Bible for guidance, we find that God's value system often contradicts what the world says. Jesus shows us that humility and service are the way to greatness in God's kingdom.

Prayer: *Dear God, guide us to live in the way your Son, Jesus, showed us. Help us to focus on humbly serving others to bring glory to you. Amen.*

Thought for the day: God defines greatness by service, not status.

John D. Bown (Minnesota, USA)

PRAYER FOCUS: THOSE WHO STRUGGLE WITH PRIDE

Bump in the night

Read Psalm 4

Weeping may stay for the night, but rejoicing comes in the morning.
Psalm 30:5 (NIV)

One night I went to bed as usual, read for a while and then went to sleep. After only around an hour a loud noise in the house suddenly woke me. I immediately ran downstairs to investigate and discovered that my large potted amaryllis had fallen over, making an awful mess. I decided I would tidy it up in the morning and went back to bed.

After that, however, I struggled to get back to sleep, tossing and turning for what seemed like hours. In the small hours of the night, things always seem worse. Something about the dark amplifies anxieties and fears. I longed for the light of the morning, and the chance to get things in perspective again.

I then recalled how many of the psalms speak to those who struggle with sleep, such as Psalm 4:8 and 30:5. Then there are those passages of scripture that show how God is our light, including one of my favourites: 'The Lord is my light and my salvation, whom shall I fear?' (Psalm 27:1). John's gospel identifies that light as Jesus – 'The light shines in the darkness but the darkness has not understood it' (John 1:5).

Today marks the spring equinox in the northern hemisphere. From this time on the night hours grow shorter and the daylight hours lengthen. Jesus came to bring light into a dark world, and even when things seem darkest, they cannot overcome the light of his presence.

Prayer: *Thank you, Lord, that you are with us at all times. May we always place our trust in you. Amen.*

Thought for the day: I can find security in God whether it is day or night.

Ann Armstrong (England, United Kingdom)

The key is love

Read Luke 6:27–36

'Do to others as you would have them do to you.'

Luke 6:31 (NRSV)

Though my colleague was a competent teacher, she seemed to have problems with everyone on campus – office staff, teachers and students. She ended up feeling lonely since most people in the school started avoiding her.

At times, we had conflicts as well. But as a Christian, I felt called to treat her with forgiveness and love. This led to her changing her attitude towards me.

Our good attitude helps other people bring out their own goodness. Jesus Christ presented the law of love, which tells us that we are to forgive, to love those who seem not to deserve it, and to pray for those we are in conflict with. This is against human nature, but we are called to do it because Christ did it first. If we treat others how we want to be treated, hardened hearts tend to soften. Love is the sign of a true Christian, and this love changes people.

Prayer: *Lord Jesus, help us to love others even when it is challenging to do so. May we treat others with respect and care. Amen.*

Thought for the day: When I treat others with care and respect, I show them Christ's love.

Amira Emmanuel (Khyber Pakhtunkhwa, Pakistan)

PRAYER FOCUS: PEOPLE I FIND HARD TO LOVE

Open doors

Read Exodus 3:7–14

So Abram departed, as the Lord had spoken unto him; and Lot went with him: and Abram was seventy and five years old when he departed out of Haran.

Genesis 12:4 (KJV)

Benji, our sweet, new foster cat had been confined to a small bedroom for eight months while he healed from injuries and countless medical conditions. He didn't quite comprehend the freedom available to him when he came to our home. My husband and I were excited to offer him open doors and countless spots to play and nap. We were therefore puzzled over Benji's choice to stay in one small room.

As I pondered his self-imposed isolation, I recognised my own tendency to limit myself to the comfortable and familiar. I often confine myself to a perceived 'safe space' without venturing out into the unknown. The Bible is filled with stories of God's urging people to be courageous. When called by God to journey to an unfamiliar place, Abram 'departed, as the Lord had spoken unto him'. Moses, too, followed God's command. God stood by both Abram and Moses and kept them safe. They would have missed an abundance of blessings had they not obeyed God's commands.

After an adjustment period, Benji is now enjoying multiple window perches and comfy chairs with warm blankets. Benji's trust in us allowed him to move beyond the familiar. May our trust in the Lord's plans allow us to do the same.

Prayer: *Dear God, help us to embrace the opportunities you provide to serve you. Thank you for being with us always. Amen.*

Thought for the day: I will be open to nudges from God to step out of my comfort zone.

Melanie Sue Fretz (Pennsylvania, USA)

 PRAYER FOCUS: SOMEONE ADJUSTING TO A NEW HOME

Give me strength

Read Isaiah 40:27–31

Come quickly to help me, my Lord and my Saviour.

Psalm 38:22 (NIV)

Sometimes I look at the day ahead of me and ask myself, *Where will I get the energy that I need?* As I ponder my situation, I think of King David. He often found himself in circumstances where he felt he did not have the strength to carry on. And he turned to God for help, like in today's quoted scripture. His cry not only expressed his feelings of despair but also his confidence that God *would* help; he had experienced God's help many times before.

Isaiah 40:31 reminds us that 'those who hope in the Lord will renew their strength. They will soar on wings like eagles; they will run and not grow weary.' God knows how we feel. God is with us every day, even though our days may be difficult. Like the air currents that enable eagles to soar, God gives us the strength and inspiration to keep going and not grow weary.

God gives me the wisdom to focus my energy on things that matter and to avoid spending time on meaningless or unhelpful activities, such as endlessly scrolling through social media posts. Not only does God give me the strength to do what I have to do, God helps me to be a better person – to treat others with respect and to have compassion on those who are struggling.

Prayer: *Dear Lord, thank you for hearing us when we cry out to you and for giving us strength and the help we need to make a difference in the world. Amen.*

Thought for the day: When I lack strength, I will turn to God and trust that God will help me.

Wolfgang Bernhardt (KwaZulu-Natal, South Africa)

PRAYER FOCUS: THOSE STRUGGLING WITH LOW ENERGY

Never give up

Read 1 Corinthians 4:9–13

My beloved brothers and sisters, be steadfast, immovable, always excelling in the work of the Lord because you know that in the Lord your labour is not in vain.

1 Corinthians 15:58 (NRSV)

As I approached the halfway house to lead a Bible study, I felt discouraged and was struggling with self-doubt. Recently, a church member had harshly criticised a sermon I preached, and I was shaken by her criticism.

Upon entering the house, I was met by one of the residents. Beaming, he handed me a card. 'This is for you,' he said. Other men from the Bible study group had gathered around to watch my response. Unknowingly, he had chosen the perfect card for what I was struggling with. Printed on the outside was 1 Corinthians 15:58. Inside he had written, 'It may be a strange way to say it, but you care. The day of our Bible study we know you will be there. You pray for us. You open the scriptures to us. You care.' How humbling. How rejuvenating. How vital it is to show up and not give up!

The apostle Paul had plenty of reasons to give up. Not only did he face sharp criticism for sharing the gospel, he was brutally beaten, cursed and slandered. Yet he kept going. It is imperative that those entrusted with the gospel prove faithful (see 1 Corinthians 4:1–2). When we feel discouraged, the Bible offers examples of people who persevered, inspiring us to do the same.

Prayer: *Dear God, thank you for encouraging us through scripture and the words of others. Give us the strength to persevere as we share your gospel. Amen.*

Thought for the day: In the face of criticism, scripture gives me courage to persevere.

Nancy K. Overgaard (Minnesota, USA)

More to the story

Read Ruth 4:1–17

The women said to Naomi: 'Praise be to the Lord, who this day has not left you without a guardian-redeemer… He will renew your life and sustain you in your old age.'

Ruth 4:14–15 (NIV)

After 25 years of teaching high school English, I was retiring. In the past three years I had experienced verbal and emotional abuse, and though I wanted to continue teaching, my mental health couldn't handle it. A career I had worked hard for and loved with my whole being was now causing tears, anxiety and doubt. I was leaving behind students who needed me, and I worried that I had let God down. Like Naomi in the book of Ruth, I was ready to give up and simply live my life out to the end in a simple fashion.

But God had something new waiting for me in my part-time work at the local library. When the library wanted to start an adult writing group, I took on the challenge – glad for something to do. In guiding the group and writing my own teaching memoirs, I have found my voice again. I now have a growing writers' group that both relies on and encourages me.

My health improved within six months of retiring, and I am happy again. When I thought I was useless and broken, God placed me where I was supposed to be. Now I know how Naomi must have felt, thinking her life was over and then holding her grandson, Obed, in her arms. Even then the story wasn't done, and neither is mine.

Prayer: *Dear God, when we feel there is no other way, help us to trust you. Help us to be open to the new paths you lay before us, and guide us as we take the next step. Amen.*

Thought for the day: God can make a way where there seems to be no way.

Kimberly Butnick (Wisconsin, USA)

From worry to worship

Read Philippians 4:10–13

Give thanks in all circumstances; for this is God's will for you in Christ Jesus.

1 Thessalonians 5:18 (NIV)

As I walked along the road one sweltering summer morning, my mind was a jumble of worries. Recent problems – property disputes, family issues and the uncertainty of the future – bore down on me like a physical force, making every step feel like a struggle with no end in sight.

Just then, I noticed an elderly man pulling a handcart loaded with scraps. His ragged clothes and weathered skin spoke of a life of hardship. Yet despite the heat and his apparent poverty, he was singing and worshipping the Lord with joy. Then I saw the words written on his handcart: 'God is Love.' Seeing someone in such a difficult situation proclaim God's love was inspiring.

That man taught me a valuable lesson. He was a living embodiment of the power of faith and trust – a stark contrast to me, stuck in my worries and fears. His example was a powerful reminder that God's love never fails. All I needed to do was learn to feel it, trust in it and let it guide me.

Prayer: *Loving God, help us to learn to be grateful and worship you in all circumstances. May we trust in your love always. Amen.*

Thought for the day: God shows up in unexpected places.

Hitesh J. Solanki (Gujarat, India)

Under his wing

Read Psalm 91

He will cover you with his feathers, and under his wings you will find refuge; his faithfulness will be your shield and rampart.
Psalm 91:4 (NIV)

About a month ago, one of my chickens went missing. I looked for her, but she was nowhere to be found. I was sad about it because she was friendly and a good egg-layer.

Two weeks later as I was leaving for work, there she was – sitting on the front porch. Reaching down to pet her, I gave her a little scolding for scaring me. Just then, a little yellow head popped up out of her feathers. The tiny creature tilted its head and peeped at me. Then another head popped out. Then another. There were five chicks all tucked up warm and safe under the generous cover of the hen's feathers. I gathered them up and took them to a safe spot and fed them. Over the next few days, I loved watching the attentive and patient mother hen tend to her tiny chicks. When it was time to rest, she would sit down and open her wings for the chicks to rest under.

Every time I watched the hen invite her babies to shelter in her feathers, I was reminded of Psalm 91. We can find peace and rest in the refuge that God offers us. Sometimes we forget that no matter what fear or weariness weighs us down, God is waiting for us to accept the invitation to come and find refuge and peace under his wings.

Prayer: *Dear Lord, fill us with your peace. Shelter us in your presence and protect us. Amen.*

Thought for the day: The Lord is my comfort and refuge.

Melissa Levi (Tennessee, USA)

PRAYER FOCUS: SOMEONE LIVING IN UNSAFE CONDITIONS

Trust in a loving parent

Read Luke 12:27–31

'Do not be afraid, little flock, for it is your Father's good pleasure to give you the kingdom.'
Luke 12:32 (NRSV)

In the weeks leading up to his tonsil surgery, our seven-year-old son was understandably anxious. He had never had surgery before and was afraid of the unknown. He asked about being put to sleep and how his throat would feel afterward. He tried to alleviate his fears by gathering information. It's scary to face the unknown and have no control over the outcome.

As my husband and I navigated how much to tell him and when, God showed me how often I find myself in this same situation. Just as we told our son we would be by his side during every step of the process, God, our loving parent, promises never to leave us. It is comforting for me to think about how God can always see the opportunities in our struggles. We sometimes have to pass through the overwhelming and the negative to reach new life on the other side.

Our son's surgery was successful, and going through that situation strengthened his relationship with God. With God's help, I will remember this and have faith the next time I face a tough road into the unknown.

Prayer: *Dear God, thank you for reminding us of your constant presence and plans for our lives. May we trust in you always. Amen.*

Thought for the day: Like a loving parent, God offers comfort and assurance as I navigate the unknown.

Melissa Webb (North Carolina, USA)

Holy week

Read John 13:31–38

Since my youth, God, you have taught me, and to this day I declare your marvellous deeds.

Psalm 71:17 (NIV)

Observing Holy Week is something new for me. In my childhood home we learned about God, but we were not strong believers. Eventually, we left God behind altogether.

My life has been filled with problems, stress, work and many other struggles. But embraced by God's mercy and strengthened by God's word and *El Aposento Alto* (the Spanish-language edition of *The Upper Room*), I've been able to find my way back to God's path.

Now after many years, I have come to see, accept and feel very different about Holy Week and what it represents: the love, grace, mercy and sacrifice of our Lord. I now realise how at the peak of Jesus' life, he showed his love for humankind. All the virtues Jesus demonstrated throughout his life showed this love. With the opportunity to write this meditation, I am putting into action the words Jesus said: 'Go home to your own people and tell them how much the Lord has done for you' (Mark 5:19).

Prayer: *Lord Jesus, we give thanks for the great love you have for each one of us. As you taught us, we pray, 'Our Father which art in heaven, Hallowed be thy name. Thy kingdom come, Thy will be done in earth, as it is in heaven. Give us this day our daily bread. And forgive us our debts, as we forgive our debtors. And lead us not into temptation, but deliver us from evil: For thine is the kingdom, and the power, and the glory, for ever. Amen' (Matthew 6:9–13, KJV).*

Thought for the day: I give praise and thanks for all the Lord has done for me.

Daniel Valencia Guevara (State of Mexico, Mexico)

PRAYER FOCUS: PEOPLE STRUGGLING TO FIND GOD AGAIN

Healing through the Psalms

Read Psalm 109:21–31

Help me, Lord my God; save me according to your unfailing love. Let them know that it is your hand, that you, Lord, have done it.
Psalm 109:26–27 (NIV)

Beneath my quiet persona I was an angry, bitter teen. I resented that I had been born into a highly dysfunctional family. I saw other healthy families and wondered why mine was not like that.

For years, even after I came to Christ as a young adult, I still wrestled with those feelings of anger and bitterness. But the Psalms gave me a way to deal with my emotions. Through these beautifully honest poems and songs, I saw many of my emotions displayed by King David. He got angry at his enemies. At times he was bitter about the circumstances of his life.

I was shocked at how vocal David was with God about how he felt. But I was also comforted. I saw that there is no emotion I cannot express to our loving Father. God can handle whatever I have to say and always listens to me.

By letting my feelings be known to God and releasing them, I found that God was able to heal my hurting heart and transform my anger and bitterness into peace, contentment and even joy. God, who is patient and kind, longs to heal and transform us and will do so no matter how long it takes.

Prayer: *Healing Father, thank you for allowing us to voice whatever emotions we have and for listening patiently and with compassion. Amen.*

Thought for the day: There are no boundaries to the emotions I can express to God.

Denise Kohlmeyer (Illinois, USA)

Love one another

Read 1 Corinthians 13:1–7

'I give you a new commandment, that you love one another. Just as I have loved you, you also should love one another. By this everyone will know that you are my disciples, if you have love for one another.'
John 13:34–35 (NRSV)

Though I have been in and out of ministry, I have struggled throughout my life with my faith in God and the institution of the Christian church. Much of the struggle is due to what I have witnessed in the church.

During my time in ministry, I have seen people turned away from churches where I served because they didn't live by certain standards. I have always felt that these churches were missing something.

I love that Jesus never demanded perfection or expected people to reach a certain standard first and then follow. Instead, Jesus met people right where they were. He still does. Jesus loves and accepts us for who we are, offering us forgiveness even when we don't ask for it.

On the cross, Jesus showed the extent of his love by forgiving the criminal hanging next to him, who asked only for Jesus to remember him. The criminal didn't ask for forgiveness; he said he deserved his punishment. But Jesus gave him the unexpected gifts of grace, mercy and forgiveness (see Luke 23:39–43). Jesus doesn't expect us to be perfect. But if we want to follow him, he expects us to love others – just as he loves us.

Prayer: *Almighty God, thank you for the gift of your Son and for loving us unconditionally. Give us the courage to love others as you love us. Amen.*

Thought for the day: I will be bold in loving others as Jesus loves me.

Ryan W. (Michigan, USA)

PRAYER FOCUS: TO SHOW GOD'S LOVE TO EVERYONE I MEET

A healthy diet

Read Romans 8:1–6

Finally, brothers and sisters, whatever is true, whatever is noble, whatever is right, whatever is pure, whatever is lovely, whatever is admirable – if anything is excellent or praiseworthy – think about such things.

Philippians 4:8 (NIV)

My medical tests and scans said everything was normal, but my symptoms persisted. Eventually, my doctor advised me to eliminate certain foods from my diet for a period of time. Within a week of doing this, my symptoms had almost disappeared. I was amazed at how changing what I ate had made such a big difference to my health.

I have noticed something similar in other areas of my life. What I take in through television, radio and other media makes a big difference in how I feel emotionally, psychologically and spiritually. Feeding on the wrong things can increase anxiety, confusion and doubts. Feeding on the right things like scripture, good literature and sermons, and starting my day with *The Upper Room* nourishes my spirit and affects my physical wellbeing. As I am learning to eliminate foods that trigger my physical symptoms, I am also learning to do the same in other areas of my life, and I feel much better for doing so.

Prayer: *Dear Lord, help us to feed our hearts and minds with good things. Nourish us with your word so that we can grow to be more like you. Amen.*

Thought for the day: Today I will nourish my spirit by reading scripture.

Miki Parsons (England, United Kingdom)

My commander

Read John 15:9–17

'You call me Teacher and Lord, and you are right, for that is what I am. So if I, your Lord and Teacher, have washed your feet, you also ought to wash one another's feet.'
John 13:13–14 (NRSV)

When I declare Jesus as my Lord and Saviour, I usually focus on the word *saviour* because I feel grateful that Jesus has saved me. But I wonder, when I call him 'Lord', what am I really saying? I researched this, and discovered that the Greek word for *lord* is *kyrios*, which can be translated as a man with great power and authority.

In the military every person must answer to someone of higher rank and obey the orders of their commander. In today's reading from the gospel of John, Jesus gives his disciples a single command: 'Love one another as I have loved you.' And he led by example, first serving the disciples by washing their feet and then demonstrating the greatest possible love – 'to lay down one's life for one's friends'.

So now when I encounter the word *Lord* in scripture or say it in prayer, I add Commander. This reminds me to obey my Lord's command – to love others through service and self-sacrifice.

Prayer: *Jesus, our Lord and Commander, help us to obey your instruction to love and serve one another as you love us. Amen.*

Thought for the day: How will I love and serve others as Christ commanded?

Steve Mills (California, USA)

Carrying the cross

Read Matthew 5:38–42

As the soldiers led him away, they seized Simon from Cyrene, who was on his way in from the country, and put the cross on him and made him carry it behind Jesus.

Luke 23:26 (NIV)

On one Good Friday, I watched a moving performance of a Passion play taking place on the street. At one point in the play, one of the Roman soldiers roughly commanded an unsuspecting audience member in the onlooking crowd to carry the cross for Jesus. The poor chap reluctantly put down the shopping bag he had with him, and stooped down to shoulder that instrument of torture. One minute, he was just a passive onlooker, the next, this man was charged with being part of the drama – a re-enactment of one of the most significant events in history.

While we are not forced to carry literal crosses, our lives can likewise take unexpected turns. Sometimes, like Simon from Cyrene, we may not have much of a choice over the situation. But usually we can choose how we respond, and with the help of the Holy Spirit, we can do so with grace. We can reply with a kind word, or walk the extra mile, or turn the other cheek.

We never will know what eternal purpose God is working out through our simple acts of obedience, but we are privileged for God to include us in the unfolding drama of God's work of redemption.

Prayer: *Dear Lord, give us the grace to respond to changes in our lives in the way that you taught us.*

Thought for the day: 'Blessed are the meek, for they will inherit the earth' (Matthew 5:5).

Hilary Allen (England, United Kingdom)

A moment of faith

Read Luke 24:13–27

'We had hoped that he was the one who was going to redeem Israel.'
Luke 24:21 (NIV)

After months of applying for jobs, I finally had a great offer! Everything seemed to be falling into place. Then suddenly, the company changed their mind. I felt lost, confused and sad. I wondered where God was in it all.

Slowly, I began to realise that this is how the disciples must have felt after Jesus' crucifixion. They had believed that Jesus was the one who was going to redeem Israel. The events of his life on earth and the miracles he had performed confirmed their hopes that the long-awaited Messiah was finally here, fulfilling the promises of scripture. Then Jesus was crucified, and all hope seemed to be gone. The disciples must have felt incredibly lost, confused and sad. It was in this moment that the disciples faced the ultimate test of their faith. Did they truly believe in God's power and Jesus' promises?

Although challenging situations may test us and cause us to question God, they can become defining moments of faith, ultimately strengthening our relationship with God. Even when we experience life's twists and turns, God is faithful to us because of who God is – a promise keeper and a miracle worker.

Prayer: *Dear Father, thank you for your presence with us as we put our hope and trust in you. Help us to notice all the ways your resurrecting power is at work in our lives. Amen.*

Thought for the day: In all circumstances, I will trust in God's faithfulness.

Connie Siedler (Auvergne-Rhône-Alpes, France)

Jesus is risen!

Read Matthew 28:1–10

The angel said to the women, 'Do not be afraid, for I know that you are looking for Jesus, who was crucified. He is not here; he has risen, just as he said.'

Matthew 28:5–6 (NIV)

When my children were very young, we attended an Easter service. While preaching about the resurrection of Jesus, the pastor talked about how Mary Magdalene and another Mary went to Jesus' tomb. They found the stone rolled back and encountered an angel of the Lord. Then the pastor asked a rhetorical question: 'What did the angel say to the women?' Surprising us all, my five-year-old daughter blurted out, 'Jesus is risen!' She said it so fervently and innocently that the pastor commented on her vigour in announcing Jesus' resurrection.

I've never forgotten that moment. My daughter had learned about Jesus' life and resurrection in Sunday school, so she knew the answer to the question and was proud to state it. I felt blessed by her enthusiastic response. We can learn from children to be witnesses of God's word, proclaiming it for all to hear. We are all God's children, and God loves us!

Prayer: *Thank you, God, for the blessing of children and all that they teach us about faith in you. Amen.*

Thought for the day: I will embrace God's love for me like a child – wholeheartedly.

Candace Kaufman (New York, USA)

 PRAYER FOCUS: THE CHILDREN IN MY CHURCH

Late bloomers

Read Luke 13:1–9

God saw all that he had made, and it was very good. And there was evening, and there was morning – the sixth day.

Genesis 1:31 (NIV)

At our local grocery store, they often have flower bargains and markdowns after the weekend rush. When I went to the store two days after Easter, there were some Easter lilies on the bargain table. Most now displayed only drooping, lifeless flowers. But there were a few that still had some unopened buds and one with no opened flowers at all. I bought that one.

A week after Easter when still no buds had opened, I wondered if it would ever bloom. But after two weeks, one of the three buds opened fully in perfect splendour. Soon all three buds had bloomed. It was beautiful.

The parable of the fig tree illustrates the patience of the gardener. The landowner wanted to chop down the tree, but the gardener said to wait another year. And God is like the gardener, waiting for the bearing of fruit and nurturing the soil. God waits and hopes for each of us to bloom. Even when we may grow frustrated by waiting, God is patient and loving, and never casts us aside.

Prayer: *O Lord, we thank you for your patient love. Thank you for always encouraging us and never giving up on us. Amen.*

Thought for the day: I will wait patiently for my time to bear fruit for the Lord.

Mike C. Bertoglio (Georgia, USA)

Living water

Read John 4:4–14

Jesus said, 'Those who drink of the water that I will give them will never be thirsty. The water that I will give will become in them a spring of water gushing up to eternal life.'
John 4:14 (NRSV)

Because of our identity, culture or background we often feel separated from other people. The Samaritan woman who spoke with Jesus at the well was different from him because of her heritage and how she viewed traditions. But Jesus chose to speak to her, teaching her about the water that gives eternal life. Not only that, Jesus would also go on to show what being set apart means. Through Jesus, the living water, we are set apart to have a new identity and life, to worship him in spirit and in truth, and to tell others about him.

Imagine the surprise among the Samaritans when the woman told them about Jesus. This woman who was on the margins of society was used by Jesus to spread the good news to those around her.

No matter what has separated us from God before, through Jesus we are set apart to worship and serve God. Let us surrender the past and dedicate ourselves to living in a way that brings glory to God as we tell others about God's mercy and grace.

Prayer: *Dear God, thank you for the living water that gives life, allowing us to serve you and tell others about you. Amen.*

Thought for the day: My life is set apart to worship God.

Paolo Rivera (National Capital Region, Philippines)

Making the rounds

Read Colossians 3:12–17

Be kind to one another, tenderhearted, forgiving one another, as God in Christ has forgiven you.

Ephesians 4:32 (NRSV)

As I watered my pothos plant, I thought of its history. The original plant was given to my mother as a housewarming gift close to 60 years earlier. When I moved into my first home, Mum gifted me with my own plant grown from a clipping. I eventually propagated another plant, which I displayed in my office.

Throughout the years, I shared clippings with other family members, friends and co-workers. When I think of all the homes that have welcomed that plant, it strikes me – it has really made the rounds! Through the years, how many people have I shared that plant with and, in turn, how many of those folks shared clippings from their plants as well?

It pleases me to know I've reached others through this act of sharing. It makes me even happier to know that a similar generosity in the recipients may keep the plant making the rounds for years to come. I hope to spark this same synergy each time I share the love of Christ through words of encouragement, a forgiving heart, a touch of compassion and a spirit full of charity. Sharing God's goodness can have far-reaching results.

Prayer: *Generous creator, may we strive to share your love each day in awareness of the far-reaching effects of our actions. Amen.*

Thought for the day: I will reach out in kindness to others – every day.

Monica A. Andermann (New York, USA)

PRAYER FOCUS: THOSE WHOSE GENEROSITY INSPIRES ME

A stranger's blessing

Read Exodus 14:10–14

'The Lord will fight for you; you need only to be still.'
Exodus 14:14 (NIV)

One Easter Sunday at 2.30 in the morning, my husband and I got a call that our 17-year-old son had been arrested. As we walked into the jail, we noticed an older man walking behind us, pulling a cooler. With tears in my eyes and a lump in my throat, I approached the reception window where a woman told us to sit down and wait. The man who had come in behind us told the woman that he was there to deliver treats for an Easter sunrise service. He proceeded inside while my husband and I waited in silence, a range of emotions stirring within us.

Then we saw the man walk out of the jail after delivering the treats. A few minutes later he walked back inside, towards us. With caring eyes, he looked at us and said, 'I don't know if you're Christians or not, but I'd like to pray with you.' Tears poured forth, but at the same time a peace overcame me. The three of us joined hands in that empty jail waiting room, and this stranger prayed for our family. Immediately, I was filled with love and peace in one of the darkest moments of my life.

God sent this man to love and comfort us when we needed it most. While it didn't make all of our troubles disappear, it reminded us that God cares for us and is with us through it all.

Prayer: *Dear Lord, thank you for your comfort in difficult times. May we be a blessing to others in their time of need. Amen.*

Thought for the day: I will pray for and comfort others when they are in need.

Lori McGonegle (Alabama, USA)

Moved by the Spirit

Read Acts 2:1–4

Suddenly a sound like the blowing of a violent wind came from heaven and filled the whole house where they were sitting.
Acts 2:2 (NIV)

Not long ago, my family and I were in Charlotte, North Carolina, and had the opportunity to visit the Discovery Place Science Museum. It had an exhibit about how sailboats are moved by the wind, complete with model boats to test.

First I placed my boat with its sail straight, and nothing happened. Then I tried again, positioning the sail another way. Still, nothing happened. My son, Ben, came up to me and said, 'You need to twist your sail and trust the wind.' I couldn't believe that a sail that wasn't straight and perfectly aligned would catch the wind well. But when I tried what he said, gently twisting the sail, the wind pushed the boat and moved it forward fast!

Many times in my life I have wanted things to be perfectly aligned and under my control. We often want things to look just right. But we need to trust that God is in control. The Holy Spirit is the wind that propels us, moving us towards God's purpose.

Prayer: *God of fire and wind, renew our strength and refresh our faith with your Spirit. May we always trust in you. Amen.*

Thought for the day: Where do I notice the Spirit moving in my life?

Daniel Contreras (Francisco Morazán, Honduras)

PRAYER FOCUS: TO BE OPEN TO LEARNING NEW THINGS

Spiritual lunch

Read Isaiah 55:1–5

'Listen, listen to me, and eat what is good, and you will delight in the richest of fare.'

Isaiah 55:2 (NIV)

I've found that it's important to spend time quietly focusing on God as the day begins and also as it ends. But what about in the middle of the day, when we're taken up with many demands?

When I was a young mother of three children, all under five, while also working from home, I would grab any brief after-lunch lull as an opportunity to read a few Bible verses and enjoy Jesus being close to me. As I did so, the children usually played on the floor around me, and I promised to join them 'as soon as my mug of coffee is empty'. How eagerly my little daughter would check on the coffee level as it slowly went down!

Those moments became so strengthening to me that I've programmed them into most days ever since. After lunch my body is satisfied, but my spirit is still thirsty and needs intake. 'I'm the only answer to that,' God indicates to us in Isaiah 55: 'Come, buy wine and milk without money and without cost… Listen to me, and eat what is good, and you will delight in the richest of fare.' Wow!

What a delight to be able to spend one-to-one time with Jesus, and then go back to a busy day in his company.

Prayer: *Dear Jesus, just us we take time for meals to nourish our bodies, help us to take time to feed on your word. Amen.*

Thought for the day: Jesus said: 'Let anyone who is thirsty come to me and drink' (John 7:37).

Elaine Brown (Scotland, United Kingdom)

Trusting God's love

Read Ephesians 3:14–21

I pray that you... grasp how wide and long and high and deep is the love of Christ.

Ephesians 3:17–18 (NIV)

My husband and I are constantly finding ways to reinforce to our adopted children that we can be trusted, that we love them and that they are safe and special. It's all the small moments of being together, connecting, reconnecting and getting through difficulties together, over and over again, that build on this message: *you can trust our love, we accept you and we are here for you*.

As Christians, we know God as the one who chose us, loved us and brought us into God's family. This loving God is one who would do anything to help us thrive and bring us near, who offers us belonging, safety and encouragement. Sometimes, for many reasons, we find it hard to trust, but God wants to spend our lifetimes showing us, over and over again, the depth of God's love and how much we can trust it.

The epistle of James says: 'Come near to God and he will come near to you' (James 4:8). Drawing closer to God, spending our lifetime connecting and reconnecting with God, taking daily steps to put our trust in God, will help us, over time, to know the depth of God's love for us.

Prayer: *Dear Lord, help us to receive and trust your love today and every day. Amen.*

Thought for the day: How can you connect with God's loving heart today?

Amy Turner (England, United Kingdom)

God's direction

Read Genesis 12:10–20

I will instruct you and teach you in the way you should go;
I will counsel you with my loving eye on you.
Psalm 32:8 (NIV)

One day while travelling to work I had to change buses. When I reached my first stop, my phone navigation indicated that my next stop was across the road and to the left. But I didn't see a bus stop on the left, so I walked to a stop I could see on the right. It wasn't the correct stop, though. I decided to trust the navigation, but when I reached my supposed destination I still didn't see a bus stop. Then I looked up and saw a sign hidden among the trees. Relieved, I caught the bus in time and made it to work.

In Genesis 12:10–20, Abram travelled with Sarai to Canaan, a land that God promised would be blessed. When Canaan experienced famine, Abram chose to go to Egypt instead. However, God remained faithful and protected Abram and Sarai, eventually leading them back to the right path.

Like Abram, when we follow God's direction, we may encounter difficulties that seem to contradict God's promises. This doesn't mean the path is wrong – rather, it is a test of our faith. Even when we face challenges, God is trustworthy. If we have faith and follow God's guidance, we will eventually reach the right place.

Prayer: *Heavenly Father, help us to put our trust in your guidance, even among hardships and uncertainty. Sometimes we cannot see the whole picture, but we know you can. Amen.*

Thought for the day: Even when I can't see the destination, I will follow God's guidance.

Preeti Stanly Thakor (New South Wales, Australia)

Faithful effort

Read Galatians 6:1–6

Each person should test their own work and be happy with doing a good job and not compare themselves with others.

Galatians 6:4 (CEB)

Several years ago, I watched a short video from a weight-lifting competition. The two competitors had to deadlift a huge amount of weight – over 200 pounds – as many times as they could within the allotted time. Whoever completed the most repetitions before time ran out won the competition.

Both men showed an outstanding display of strength and endurance. However, when the first man reached his limit, he responded in a way that impressed me. He quickly turned to the competitor who had bested him and cheered for him to keep going! With his amazing performance and his highly respectful sportsmanship, the man who lost the competition showed how big and strong he was – literally and figuratively.

Sometimes in our walk with Jesus Christ, our effort in pursuing a goal doesn't yield the success we want. Thankfully, in Christ Jesus, our effort is never in vain when we embrace God's grace and mercy. We have no need to be ashamed when we've given our all and done what we can to glorify God.

Prayer: *Dear heavenly Father, thank you for loving and caring for us at all times. In Jesus' name we pray. Amen.*

Thought for the day: My faithful effort is more important than earthly success.

Tyler Myers (Ohio, USA)

Words linger

Read Ephesians 4:22–29

Do not let any unwholesome talk come out of your mouths, but only what is helpful for building others up according to their needs, that it may benefit those who listen.

Ephesians 4:29 (NIV)

When an older salesperson in a cosmetics department asked me what I used to cleanse my face, as a naive 20-year-old with blemish-free, youthful skin I was flattered. I proudly named the hand soap I used. She grimaced and harshly predicted, 'When you are 40 you will look 80!' I felt humiliated by her criticism, and though I quickly walked away, the sting of her words stayed with me. Words can and do find permanent residence in us. Words have long-lasting power.

This deep-rooted memory of the salesperson prompts and encourages me to be mindful and to guard my words. The Bible offers wisdom regarding the words we speak. Ecclesiastes 10:12 says, 'Words from the mouth of the wise are gracious.' In today's verse Paul directs believers to speak politely, while in Colossians 4:6 he writes that conversations need to be characterised by grace and wisdom. Because words can live on and either damage or uplift the human spirit, we need to speak cautiously and carefully so we bring out the best in others. May we give grace to those listening, building up others through all our conversations.

Prayer: *Dear God, may our words be acceptable and bring healing to the listener, help to the hurting and support to the weary. Amen.*

Thought for the day: My words have the power to build up or tear down. Which will I choose?

Beverly Taylor (Arizona, USA)

 PRAYER FOCUS: SOMEONE WHOSE WORDS HAVE DEEPLY AFFECTED ME

Calm in the storm

Read Luke 8:22–25

Peace I leave with you; my peace I give to you.

John 14:27 (NRSV)

After an early morning departure, all I wanted was some much-needed rest on the plane. But as we took off, the pilot announced there would be turbulence. When the first wave hit, it felt like I was jerked out of my seat – a rude awakening. I was determined to sleep but found it incredibly difficult as the plane swayed and jolted.

I thought of the story where Jesus slept through a storm on a boat. I wondered, *How did Jesus manage to sleep through such chaos?* In that moment, I began to grasp the concept of peace that 'surpasses all understanding' (Philippians 4:7). Despite the plane's violent movements, when I focused inward I noticed a remarkable sense of peace. I realised that peace doesn't mean the absence of troubles. Rather, it is a conscious choice to remain calm amid the storm. But we cannot do this alone, and that is why Christ gave us his peace.

When we face storms, saying a prayer or affirmation can be grounding. Philippians 4:6–7 tells us that prayer can bring a peace that transcends understanding. Amid turbulence, let us remember that Christ's peace has been given to us – a gift we can freely accept.

Prayer: *Dear God, help us to embrace the gift of your peace even in the most difficult times. Amen.*

Thought for the day: I can have peace in my heart because God is with me in the storm.

Lilian Okafor (Lagos, Nigeria)

God of all

Read Matthew 22:23–33

Have ye not read that which was spoken unto you by God, saying, I am the God of Abraham, and the God of Isaac, and the God of Jacob?
Matthew 22:31–32 (KJV)

Recently, I read Matthew 22, where Jesus quotes Exodus to the Sadducees who were questioning him. In the Old Testament, many people gain new names. For example, Abram becomes Abraham and Jacob becomes Israel. In the quote in Matthew 22:32, we have Abraham's new name, Isaac (whose name never changed), and Jacob's old name. With that in mind, another way I read the scripture is like this: I am the God of who you *will be* (Abraham), the God of who you *are* (Isaac), and the God of who you *used to be* (Jacob).

Have you ever thought of your life's timeline in terms of your faith – before Christ and after Christ? We try to give grace for today and have faith for tomorrow, but sometimes we allow regret to reign over yesterday. We look back and see only our mistakes and failures. It was the heartache in Jacob's life that led him to wrestle with the angel and receive his new name. But even after his name changed, God called him Jacob when God spoke to Moses out of the burning bush (see Exodus 3:1–6, 13–16), which is what Jesus quotes in Matthew 22. It's as if God were saying, 'I'm not just God of the new you; I'm God of the old you too!'

I'm thankful God is the God of who we are and who we're becoming – and also the God of who we were.

Prayer: *Dear Lord, you are the God of yesterday, today and tomorrow. Help us to see your grace in every stage of our lives. Amen.*

Thought for the day: God's love for me is timeless.

Jacob P. Stump (Texas, USA)

Stitched on my heart

Read Psalm 119:169–176

Your word is a lamp for my feet, a light on my path.
Psalm 119:105 (NIV)

I come from a long line of craftspeople. My mum was an extraordinary seamstress, and my grandmother made beautiful needlework designs. One day Mum decided it was time for me to take up the family tradition of crafting. She bought me a simple embroidery kit and taught me the basics of stitching and how to fill in a piece of fabric with differently coloured thread. The kit included a pattern to sew an image of the Bible with a candle and the words of Psalm 119:105. As I stitched the letters, the words were 'sewn' into my heart.

Psalm 119 speaks to the wisdom, beauty and blessings of God's word. The psalmist reminds us that those who follow God's ways are blessed. Over the course of the psalm we are told that God's word helps us to live honourably, gives us strength, gives us perspective and provides hope. We are told that God's word is righteous, trustworthy and everlasting.

In verse 176, the psalmist writes, 'I have strayed like a lost sheep. Seek your servant, for I have not forgotten your commands.' Similarly, I have lost my way a few times in life. I've found myself in dark, scary places. But in those moments, I remembered the words of Psalm 119:105, and I knew where to find the light. I often go back to this verse for comfort and guidance. Indeed, it is stitched on my heart. God's word is my light.

Prayer: *Holy Father, teach us your truths and guide us by your light. Amen.*

Thought for the day: Scriptures I have memorised guide me when I am in need.

Dorcas Beth Andrews (Alabama, USA)

More than enough

Read Matthew 6:24–34

'No one can serve two masters. Either you will hate the one and love the other, or you will be devoted to the one and despise the other. You cannot serve both God and money.'

Matthew 6:24 (NIV)

It's not every day that you find a gift of fresh fish right outside your house. But there they were. I had been fretting about not having enough money, but through those fish, it was as if God were saying, 'See? I can provide for your needs, so why worry?'

I was reminded of Matthew 6:25–34, and my mind was put at ease for a time. But eventually I was caught in another whirlwind of worries. That's when God pointed me to a deeper truth: I had been putting my trust in money, not in God.

In Matthew 6:24, Jesus said, 'No one can serve two masters… You cannot serve both God and money.' At first I couldn't accept that money was my master, but as I thought about it, I knew it was true. Despite having a stable job and some savings, I still worried. I focused on money, losing sight of who God is and how God has consistently provided.

I'm grateful God steered my focus back to God and reminded me of God's generous provision (see Matthew 7:11). God is my great reward, my all in all (see Genesis 15:1). And God is more than enough.

Prayer: *Dear God, forgive us when we forget that you are our all in all. Help us to find satisfaction in you alone. Amen.*

Thought for the day: No amount of riches compares to the treasure of my relationship with God.

Abigail Roque (Bulacan, Philippines)

Balm for the broken-hearted

Read Psalm 34:15–22

The Lord is close to the broken-hearted and saves those who are crushed in spirit.

Psalm 34:18 (NIV)

The weeks leading up to the anniversary of my mother's death are filled with memories. My mother's laughter, the way her eyes sparkled with kindness, the sound of her voice, and her comforting embrace are vivid in my mind. Yet the pain of her absence feels as fresh as the day she passed away. Each memory is a bittersweet reminder of the love that endures in her absence.

One evening, as I struggled with the weight of my sorrow, I opened my Bible and came across Psalm 34:18. It felt like a personal reminder that God is intimately aware of my pain. This verse assured me that my broken heart is not beyond God's reach; God is present, ready to heal and restore.

I find comfort in knowing that God is near. God understands my pain and is my constant source of strength. Even in the valley of grief, there is hope and light. My mother's memory lives on, and her spirit is a testament to the enduring love that binds us.

Grief, though heavy, is a testament to the depth of our love. And God's comforting presence is a beacon of hope, guiding us through our sorrow and into God's everlasting peace.

Prayer: *Heavenly Father, as we grieve, comfort us with your promise to be close to the broken-hearted. Strengthen our spirit, and remind us of your hope and peace. Amen.*

Thought for the day: God's presence is a balm for my broken heart.

Sean Ewing (Minnesota, USA)

Blanket of blessing

Read 1 Kings 19:15–21

So Elijah went from there and found Elisha son of Shaphat. He was ploughing with twelve yoke of oxen, and he himself was driving the twelfth pair. Elijah went up to him and threw his cloak around him.

1 Kings 19:19 (NIV)

Years ago I was invited to a nearby church as a guest preacher for Sunday worship. After my sermon, the deacon who was leading the service invited me to kneel at the altar with her for prayer.

What happened next surprised me. She took a very soft and smooth woollen blanket and covered my shoulders as she said, 'This hand-knitted blanket was given to the congregation as a special blanket of the Lord's blessing. I therefore cover our guest speaker with God's love.'

I still feel the wonderful, spiritual warmth from that blanket as I was covered in God's grace. I recalled the story of how Elijah threw his cloak around Elisha as a token of the Lord's call to be a prophet. I do not consider myself a prophet, but I know that our Lord and Saviour covers all of us in blankets of blessings. For me, the words of Numbers 6:24–26 capture this promise perfectly: 'The Lord bless you and keep you; the Lord make his face shine on you and be gracious to you; the Lord turn his face towards you and give you peace.'

Prayer: *Dear God, open our hearts to your love and grace this day and in all the days to come. In the name of Jesus we pray. Amen.*

Thought for the day: When do I feel most connected to God's love?

Øystein Brinch (Vestfold, Norway)

God's creation

Read Genesis 1:20–31

How many are your works, Lord! In wisdom you made them all; the earth is full of your creatures.
Psalm 104:24 (NIV)

One year when Earth Day fell on a Sunday, my husband and I attended a sermon at the local zoo. As we sat outdoors listening to the pastor preach about the creation story in Genesis, we could see several animals in their nearby enclosures. The pastor preached on good stewardship of our planet Earth and all its creatures, while in the background a cacophony of animal noises seemed to be proclaiming, 'God created us!'

When the pastor concluded his sermon, he encouraged us to visit God's creatures at the zoo and to learn about the zoo's conservation mission. We saw a huge variety of creatures! Moreover, we learned that many of these mammals, birds and amphibians are endangered due to habitat loss, poaching, pollution and climate change. We also learned about conservation efforts to save them.

That visit to a zoo on Earth Day inspired me to praise God for the wonders of creation. May we all do our part to protect the creatures God has entrusted to our care.

Prayer: *Creator God, thank you for this amazing planet and the creatures that inhabit it. Help us to respond by being good stewards. Amen.*

Thought for the day: How is God calling me to care for creation?

Debra Pierce (Massachusetts, USA)

Moulded by God

Read Jeremiah 18:1–6

'Like clay in the hand of the potter, so are you in my hand.'
Jeremiah 18:6 (NIV)

I am drawn to a TV competition programme involving twelve amateur potters. Each week, they are set two testing challenges, at the end of which one of them is eliminated from the competition. As is usual with this format of programme, much of the drama comes as a result of things not turning out the way the potter envisioned, often with the clay not forming the shape the potter wants.

In the book of Jeremiah, God tells the prophet to go and observe a potter at work. There Jeremiah sees that the potter is not satisfied with the pot he is making, so he reforms it on the wheel and shapes it to his liking. The message to Israel, and to us, is that we are like the clay in the hand of the potter.

We can feel like the pot that Jeremiah saw – 'marred in his hands' (v. 4): damaged, unusable and seemingly beyond repair. But our creator God, as the master potter, can remould each one of us. God has no qualms in slapping us back on the wheel, re-centring us and forming each one of us into the person God wants us to be. This may not be an exercise we would necessarily relish. But by God's amazing power, the result is a beautiful work of art.

Prayer: *Heavenly Father, take us, mould us and fill us, but most of all use us as a vessel in your service. Amen.*

Thought for the day: The good work God started in me, God will carry on to completion (see Philippians 1:6).

John Hauselman (England, United Kingdom)

Transforming light

Read Matthew 27:45–56

The light shines in the darkness, and the darkness doesn't extinguish the light.

John 1:5 (CEB)

Skyscrapers cast cold shadows through my drive downtown to work on Good Friday. An occasional intersection crossing, however, allowed a brief blast of sunlight. My mind drifted as I drove. Darkness had plagued our family for so long, and I had clung to the small glimmers of hope that broke through.

Turning west, I sat in awe as the sun's reflection against a mirrored skywalk scattered rays of light everywhere, bouncing off the windowpanes of an old brick building nearby to yet another glass structure. It made the sun appear to be shining from every direction. I was surrounded by incredible brilliance and felt a sense of peace come over me.

The old buildings downtown had seemed drab and worn-out, but in the light they had a new radiance. On Easter Sunday, the darkness of Jesus' crucifixion gave way to glory in our risen Saviour. Similarly, Jesus can take our broken-down lives and transform them. No matter our struggles, the Son is all around us!

Prayer: *Thank you, Lord Jesus, for embracing us with your peace. Help us remember that your light shines through even our darkest moments. Amen.*

Thought for the day: No matter the darkness, God's light never fades.

Lori A. Geppert (Iowa, USA)

PRAYER FOCUS: FAMILIES WHO NEED HOPE

Anowa Chipisala'cho

Read John 16:16–28

Jesus went on to say, 'In a little while you will see me no more, and then after a little while you will see me.'

John 16:16 (NIV)

I am a citizen of the Chickasaw Nation of Oklahoma, and I lead an annual mission trip that immerses participants in Native American culture while serving Native churches in Oklahoma. At the end of each trip, I remind the group that there is no definitive 'goodbye' in Native culture, only 'until I see you again'. No matter how hard it is to part, we believe that we will indeed see one another again, either in this life or the next.

In the Chickasaw language, the phrase for 'until I see you again' is *anowa chipisala'cho* (ah-noh-wah chi-pee-sah-lah-choh). This phrase is always spoken with confidence and a deeply rooted faith that we will see one another again.

Jesus' words about seeing him again can be as confusing to us as they were for the disciples, who were filled with questions about what Jesus meant. But Jesus encourages the disciples to keep a heavenly focus. Although losing Jesus was painful, Christ offered the disciples a life-giving, hope-filled promise: they would see him again. No matter how great our loss, there is always hope, grace, resurrection and a great reunion. May we always find it in our hearts to say '*anowa chipisala'cho*' because we will see one another again!

Prayer: *Aba Bini'li – creator of all things – we are thankful that 'goodbye' is not the only way, because you offer us grace and hope for our future life. Amen.*

Thought for the day: How can I live into an *anowa chipisala'cho* spirit of hope today?

Chad T. Johnson (Texas, USA)

God our Father

Read Psalm 68:4–10

A father to the fatherless, a defender of widows, is God in his holy dwelling.
Psalm 68:5 (NIV)

My father and mother separated when I was eight years old. My mum raised me and my brother, but we had very few childhood memories of our dad. The steady father figure in our lives was our grandpa, whom we called Daddy.

Daddy loved Jesus, and his life exemplified his faith. He was our go-to person for wise advice. We enjoyed listening to his personal anecdotes, and his fatherly presence was a source of comfort and confidence for me.

When Daddy passed away, I was overcome with grief and an intense feeling of being fatherless. Although I was comforted knowing that he was with Jesus, I couldn't help but feel weighed down by the pain and heartache of losing a loved one. In a quiet moment with the Lord, I remembered the phrase 'a father to the fatherless' in the Bible. I felt God assuring me then that although I had lost an earthly father – for a second time – God is my heavenly Father.

I'm grateful to God for my grandpa's presence in my life. Even though losing him has been painful, it is also an opportunity to find comfort in my heavenly Father, who is always present and faithful to me.

Prayer: *Dear God, help us to know and feel that you are near to us. May we know you as our ever-present Father, whom we can turn to and confide in. Amen.*

Thought for the day: God is my Father and protector.

Quennie Joyce Ibarra (Misamis Occidental, Philippines)

PRAYER FOCUS: THOSE WITHOUT A FATHER FIGURE

People of resurrection

Read Romans 6:1–10

If we have been united with him in a death like his, we will certainly also be united with him in a resurrection like his.

Romans 6:5 (NIV)

Every year I have a vegetable garden. I start by planting tomato and pepper seeds in pots inside the house months before the ground warms up. That way, when I transfer them out to the garden, they are already quite large. This year, I put the pots in the garage instead of the house. After several weeks, there were no sprouts. I planted more seeds and still no sprouts appeared. I gave up hope; but then when the weather warmed up, I saw sprouts in my pots. The garage had been too cold for the seeds to germinate.

How often do our dreams seem to go nowhere? When it looks like hope has been crushed and everything is bleak, we are tempted to admit defeat. But we are not a people of hopelessness and despair; we are people of resurrection. On Easter morning, the stone was rolled away, and the risen Christ stepped out leaving the grave clothes behind. That is our hope and assurance. Our trials are not the final story. Rather, trials provide a chance for a new start. Because of Jesus we are not defeated; we are people of resurrection.

Prayer: *Lord Jesus, strengthen us as we weather our trials so that we may live into the promise of resurrection. Amen.*

Thought for the day: When I face problems, the power of God renews my hope.

Bob LaForge (New Jersey, USA)

The little we offer

Read John 6:1–14

Each of you should give what you have decided in your heart to give, not reluctantly or under compulsion, for God loves a cheerful giver.
2 Corinthians 9:7 (NIV)

One night, my 10-year-old son and I were returning from another city, and we stopped to buy him some food. The eatery was crowded, but we waited patiently and I got him a rice bowl with chicken. Because it was getting late, we returned to our car, planning for him to eat on the way. Suddenly a child ran up to us with her hand held out, begging for money. Without thinking twice, my son pressed the food parcel into her hands.

In that moment I was reminded of another generous boy who gave his meal of five small loaves of bread and two small fish to Jesus when there was a crowd of 5,000 hungry people to feed. The boy didn't keep it for himself, though he must have been tired and hungry too. Jesus thanked God for the food, and it was sufficient. There were even leftovers! My son didn't solve all the problems of children living on the streets of India – or even for that one child. He just did what he could. If we all are generous in a small way, the Lord will take the little we offer and multiply it.

Prayer: *Dear God, help us to reach out to others with all that we have, even when we have only a small contribution to make. Amen.*

Thought for the day: Small, kind gestures done in the name of Jesus make a big difference.

Carol Peter (Gujarat, India)

Faith in uncertainty

Read Matthew 6:9–13

Therefore do not worry about tomorrow, for tomorrow will worry about itself. Each day has enough trouble of its own.

Matthew 6:34 (NIV)

A few years ago, I faced a period of profound uncertainty. My job situation was unstable, and I was unsure how I would support my family. Each day brought new challenges and questions without clear answers.

Sitting at the kitchen table one evening with bills scattered around us, my wife and I prayed together. As we prayed, I looked out the window and saw a small bird perched on a branch, singing joyfully. Here was a creature with no means to plan for the future, yet it seemed completely content and provided for. This reminded me of Jesus' message about the birds of the air in Matthew 6.

The next morning I took a walk to clear my mind and reflect on God's words. I noticed the beauty all around me: the flowers blooming by the roadside, the gentle rustling of leaves, and the warmth of the sun on my face. These small blessings reminded me that God cares deeply for all creation. Focusing on the present and trusting God with my future gave me a profound sense of peace.

I learned to pray daily for my needs and to leave my worries with God. This practice didn't remove the uncertainties, but it transformed how I navigated them. I began to see each day as an opportunity to witness God's faithfulness and provision, even in the smallest of things.

Prayer: *Dear heavenly Father, thank you for your constant care and provision. Teach us to live in the present and to trust in your faithfulness each day. Amen.*

Thought for the day: Day by day, I will trust in God's faithful provision.

Preston Riffe (Kentucky, USA)

 PRAYER FOCUS: THOSE FACING JOB INSECURITY

In the gap

Read Ezekiel 22:23–30

'I looked for someone among them who would build up the wall and stand before me in the gap on behalf of the land so I would not have to destroy it, but I found no one.'
Ezekiel 22:30 (NIV)

Last summer while my husband and I were walking our dog, we noticed a hollyhock plant growing on the edge of the street. The plant stood tall, tucked in a space where two concrete curb sections came together. It was an unusual place to find a flower growing.

Over the summer, I marvelled as the plant bloomed with pink flowers, attracting butterflies and affecting the whole neighbourhood. Bike riders moved to the centre of the street to avoid bumping the flowering plant. Neighbours congregated near it and watered the hollyhock. On trash pick-up day, I nervously watched the approaching garbage truck. My fluttering stomach calmed as I saw the truck swing wide around the plant.

This little plant brought to my mind the story in Ezekiel 22 of God searching for people in Jerusalem willing to stand in the gap in the wall. God was looking for people willing to make a difference and stand strong against sin when no one else would.

God still searches for people willing to stand up and make a difference. It may mean doing the unpopular or the uncomfortable. It may mean going to unexpected places or speaking to someone who seems unapproachable. It surely means trusting completely in the one who is always dependable.

Prayer: *Dear God, show us how to stand in the gap and make a difference with you and for you. Amen.*

Thought for the day: How am I being called to stand in the gap?

Helen Dening (New York, USA)

Small group questions

7 January

1 Recall a time when you felt led to reach out to someone. What did you do? How did your interactions with that person affect them and you? What did you learn?

2 Why do you think it is so important to look for ways to connect with the people around you? How do you remain open to opportunities to connect with others?

3 When have you seen God working through your small actions to make a difference? How does it encourage you to know that God can use even our smallest acts to bring love to those around us?

4 What spiritual practices help you pay attention to the movement of the Holy Spirit in your life? How does remaining aware of the Holy Spirit help you become an instrument of God's love?

5 Who in your life is lonely or in need of connection today? How can you reach out to them?

14 January

1 When have you felt abandoned? Where do you find hope when you feel alone or abandoned?

2 How does your faith help you when you have been wronged by someone? What scripture passages help you find forgiveness and a new perspective?

3 What Bible verses remind you that God cares for you and will always have more than enough for us? How do these verses encourage you and draw you closer to God?

4 Who in scripture besides Esau serves as an example of having enough despite difficult circumstances? What can you learn from their story?

5 List some examples of how God's provision and generosity have filled the places of disappointment in your life.

21 January

1 Why do you think time spent in nature experiencing creation refreshes the mind, body and soul for so many people? What other places bring you rest and rejuvenation?

2 When have you noticed something growing and thriving in unfavourable conditions? What did you think about it? What deeper ideas or lessons did it bring up for you?

3 Recall a time when you were unable to choose your situation. How did you respond? Were you able to grow in your circumstances anyway? Why or why not?

4 Why do you think we often struggle to praise and worship God when we don't like our circumstances? What helps you to glorify God in all situations?

5 Who in scripture praised and glorified God despite not getting a say in their situation? How does their example inspire you to do the same?

28 January

1 How have the people around you helped you during a time of grief? When others are experiencing grief, what do you do to help them?

2 When has someone's presence comforted you? Why was their presence so comforting?

3 Have you ever found that there were no words to help someone? What did you do instead? Why do you think words are sometimes not what a person needs?

4 How does God's presence comfort you in times of grief? What prayers and spiritual practices help you lean into God's presence?

5 Who in your life is grieving? How will you offer them your presence and comfort today?

4 February

1 Do you have a strong sense of fairness? How does your sense of fairness change depending on the situation? Why do you think we so often desire fairness?

2 Do you find that your sense of fairness is usually based on limiting factors? Do you feel the same desire for fairness when resources are abundant? Why or why not?

3 When you hear the story of the vineyard workers, do you agree with today's writer that their payment initially seems unfair? What can you learn from the answer Jesus gives regarding God's generosity?

4 How are you encouraged to know that God's grace is inexhaustible? In what ways does that knowledge help you to remain connected to God and to show grace to others?

5 What scripture passages most remind you of the abundant grace of God? How do these verses help you when you are tempted to think of God's grace as a limited resource?

11 February

1 Have you ever asked someone to pray for you and had them pray right there on the spot? If so, what was that experience like? If not, how do you think it would make you feel for someone to pray for you as soon as you asked?

2 Do you find it hard to remember prayer requests after the fact? Why or why not? What tools and methods do you use to remind yourself of prayer requests that you receive throughout the week?

3 When have you adopted a new prayer practice based on the practices of someone else? How did that new practice make a difference in your prayer life?

4 Do you ever offer to pray with others in the moment? If so, what gives you the courage to do so? If not, what might help you get better at praying in the moment?

5 What does it mean to you to pray without ceasing? How do you make prayer a consistent part of your life?

18 February

1 Have you ever attended a performance where the performers made a mistake? How did they handle the mistake? Did they get a chance for a fresh start?

2 How do you feel after you read Isaiah 43:18–19? In what ways do those verses help you avoid dwelling on your past?

3 When has God done a new thing in your life? How did that new start make a difference for you?

4 Do you struggle to let go of the past? Why or why not? How does your relationship with God give you the courage to let go of the past and embrace the present?

5 What are you surrendering to God this Lenten season? How does looking to God help you release your past and move on to a better future?

25 February

1 Have you ever been unable to go forward to receive Communion? If so, what happened? If not, what do you think you would do in that situation?

2 When have you been blessed by the care and consideration of those around you? What did they do? How did their actions make a difference for you?

3 Have you ever had a moment when you experienced Communion more deeply or in a new way? What was the situation? How did this change the way you thought about your faith or the meaning of Communion?

4 When have you experienced what it means to be a part of the body of Christ? How does being a member of the body keep you connected with your faith and your community?

5 What scripture verses most remind you of the importance of Christian community? How do you strive to be a caring and loving member of your faith community?

4 March

1 Have you ever taken notice of Matthew 14:14 where it says that Jesus had compassion on the crowd? How does that verse change the way you think about Jesus feeding the 5,000?

2 Do you think it was easy for Jesus to have compassion on the crowd? Why or why not?

3 Why do you think it can be easy for us to miss parts of familiar Bible stories when we read them quickly? What Bible story have you recently gained a new perspective on? What is the new perspective?

4 What situations and circumstances make it hard for you to show compassion to others? How does your faith help you to show compassion to others even in moments when it is challenging?

5 What scripture passages most remind you of the importance of compassion? How do these verses help you to be more compassionate each day?

11 March

1 Have you ever gone snorkelling? If so, what was it like? If not, what other activities allow you to look beyond the ordinary and witness something beautiful?

2 Recall a time when you have had a joyful experience but were unable to share it with others. Why couldn't you share it?

3 Why do you think some people are content floating on the surface, never diving deeper into a relationship with Christ? What do they miss out on?

4 How does studying scripture deepen your faith and bring you closer to God? What other spiritual practices draw you into a closer relationship with God?

5 How has the Holy Spirit helped you to realise who you are in Christ? How does your faith change the way you view and experience the world?

18 March

1 What makes weeds so persistent? Why do you think they get out of control quickly while cultivated plants often grow slowly and need more attention?

2 Today's writer draws a connection between her gardening and our lives. What in nature do you think best mirrors our lives? Why?

3 In what ways have the fruit of the Spirit helped to get rid of the 'weeds' within you? Who or what has helped you remove those weeds?

4 What scripture verses encourage you as you work to cultivate the fruit of God's Spirit? How do these verses help you keep the weeds in your life from taking over?

5 How does it help you to have a Gardener working alongside you as you remove the weeds in your life? How do you think this 'weeding' would be different if you were on your own?

25 March

1 When has something you loved turned into a source of pain or anxiety? What happened? How did you feel when that shift occurred?

2 When have you worried that you let God down? What helps you when you feel that way?

3 Who in scripture do you most relate to right now? What do you relate to most about their story? How does their story give you hope?

4 When have you experienced a difficult life change, only to find that God had something new for you? How did that experience change your relationship with God?

5 How are you encouraged to know that your story is not over, even in moments when it feels like it might be? How does scripture help you to trust that God is near and can use you regardless of your circumstances?

1 April

1 When has a diet change made a difference in how you felt? Why do you think what we eat has such an impact on our bodies?

2 Do you notice that what you take in makes a difference in how you feel emotionally, psychologically and spiritually? What makes you feel better? What makes you feel worse?

3 What roles do scripture, devotionals, sermons and other resources play in your life? What differences do you notice when you make time each day for those good things?

4 How do you know when your spirit is nourished? How do you know when it is not? What do you do when you feel that you are being worn down?

5 Who or what in your life helps you remember to nourish your spirit?

8 April

1 Do you enjoy growing and propagating plants? Why or why not?

2 What item has 'made the rounds' in your community? In what way has it made the rounds? What deeper lesson can you learn from this?

3 When have you noticed that one person's sharing sparks others to share as well? Why do you think this is?

4 In what ways do you share the love of Christ? How do you think sharing Christ's love in these ways leads to others also sharing that love?

5 What verses most encourage you to share with others? What verses encourage you to share the love of Christ? How do these verses push you to share even when you feel hesitant?

15 April

1 Recall someone's words that have taken up permanent residence in you. What are those words? Why have they had such a lasting impact on you?

2 What experiences have shown you the importance of guarding your words? How do you pull from those experiences in your interactions now?

3 What do you think characterises wise and gracious words?

4 Who in scripture would you say best exemplifies using their words cautiously and carefully? Why did you choose this person? What can you learn from them?

5 Who has built you up with their words recently? What did they say? How have you used your words to build others up recently?

22 April

1 Have you ever attended a sermon in a zoo or some other unconventional location? If so, what was it like? If not, recall a time when you worshipped or prayed in a way that was new.

2 When you see, hear or feel animals and other parts of nature, what do you think about? Do they remind you of the glory of God's creative work? What else do they bring to mind for you?

3 Which parts of creation do you find the most awe-inspiring? Why? What do we need to do to protect and preserve these parts of creation?

4 What conservation efforts are happening around you? Are you contributing to these efforts? How do you care for creation each day?

5 Do you think humans care for creation like we should? Why or why not? What changes do you think we need to make? How can we be better stewards of the earth?

29 April

1 When have you faced a time of uncertainty? How did you respond?

2 Recall a time when something in nature gave you clarity about a situation you were experiencing. What happened?

3 In what ways does spending time in nature help you to feel God's presence? How does knowing that God cares for all of creation help you to trust that God also cares for you?

4 What scripture passages and prayers help you to focus on the present and leave your worries to God?

5 Where have you witnessed God's faithful provision today? How do you stay mindful of both the big and the small ways God provides for us daily?

Journal page

Journal page

Journal page

Become a Friend of BRF Ministries

and give regularly to support our ministry

We help people of all ages to grow in faith

We encourage and support individual Christians and churches as they serve and resource the changing spiritual needs of communities today.

Anna Chaplaincy for older people

Through **Anna Chaplaincy** we're enabling churches to provide spiritual care to older people

BRF Resources

Through **BRF Resources** we're nurturing faith and resourcing lifelong discipleship

Messy Church

Through **Messy Church** we're helping churches to reach out to families

parenting for faith®

Through **Parenting for Faith** we're supporting parents as they raise their children in the Christian faith

Our ministry is only possible because of the generous support of individuals, churches, trusts and gifts in wills.

As we look to the future and make plans, **regular donations make a huge difference** in ensuring we can both start and finish projects well.

By becoming a Friend and giving regularly to our ministry, you are partnering with us in the gospel and helping change lives.

How your gift makes a difference

£2 a month	Helps us to give away **BRF Resources** via food banks and chaplaincy services	**£10** a month	Helps us to support parents and churches running the **Parenting for Faith** course
£5 a month	Helps us to support **Messy Church** volunteers and grow the wider network	**£20** a month	Helps us to develop the reach of **Anna Chaplaincy** and improve spiritual care for older people

How to become a Friend of BRF Ministries

Online – set up a Direct Debit donation at **brf.org.uk/donate** or find out how to set up a Standing Order at **brf.org.uk/friends**

By post – complete and return the form opposite to 'Freepost BRF' (*no other address or stamp is needed*)

If you have any questions, or if you want to change your regular donation or stop giving in the future, do get in touch.

Contact the fundraising team

Email: **giving@brf.org.uk**
Tel: +44 (0)1235 462305
Post: Fundraising team, BRF Ministries,
15 The Chambers, Vineyard,
Abingdon OX14 3FE

Registered with FUNDRAISING REGULATOR

SHARING OUR VISION – MAKING A GIFT

I would like to make a donation to support BRF Ministries.
Please use my gift for:

☐ Where it is most needed ☐ Anna Chaplaincy ☐ BRF Resources
☐ Messy Church ☐ Parenting for Faith

Title	First name/initials	Surname
Address		
		Postcode
Email		
Telephone		
Signature		Date

Please accept my gift of:

☐ £2 ☐ £5 ☐ £10 ☐ £20 Other £ ☐

by (*delete as appropriate*):

☐ Cheque/Charity Voucher payable to 'BRF'

☐ MasterCard/Visa/Debit card/Charity card

Name on card

Card no. ☐☐☐☐ ☐☐☐☐ ☐☐☐☐ ☐☐☐☐

Expires end M M Y Y

Signature	Date

Please complete other side of this form ➲

SHARING OUR VISION – MAKING A GIFT

BRF Ministries Gift Aid Declaration

In order to Gift Aid your donation, you must tick the box below.

☐ I want to Gift Aid my donation and any donation I make in the future or have made in the past four years to BRF Ministries

I am a UK taxpayer and understand that if I pay less Income Tax and/or Capital Gains Tax in the current tax year than the amount of Gift Aid claimed on all my donations, it is my responsibility to pay any difference.

Please notify BRF Ministries if you want to cancel this Gift Aid declaration, change your name or home address, or no longer pay sufficient tax on your income and/or capital gains.

You can also give online at **brf.org.uk/donate**, which reduces our administration costs, making your donation go further.

Our ministry is only possible because of the generous support of individuals, churches, trusts and gifts in wills.

☐ I would like to leave a gift to BRF Ministries in my will.
Please send me further information.

☐ I would like to find out about giving a regular gift to BRF Ministries.

For help or advice regarding making a gift, please contact our fundraising team +44 (0)1235 462305

Your privacy

We will use your personal data to process this transaction. From time to time we may send you information about the work of BRF Ministries that we think may be of interest to you. Our privacy policy is available at **brf.org.uk/privacy**. Please contact us if you wish to discuss your mailing preferences.

Registered with FUNDRAISING REGULATOR

Please complete other side of this form

Please return this form to 'Freepost BRF'

No other address information or stamp is needed

BRF

Bible Reading Fellowship is a charity (233280) and company limited by guarantee (301324), registered in England and Wales

After a gruelling 140-mile pilgrimage walking across the rugged terrain of North Wales, Trystan Owain Hughes finds himself facing another, very different pilgrimage as he recovers from a serious injury sustained on the walk. In *To Hell's Mouth and Back* he explores his experience of suffering, considering how God can redeem and transform pain and disability, and examines how common experiences of pilgrimage are echoed in the challenges of our life journeys. Along the way, the reader is led to consider the journeys we all face, as we search for God's presence in our joys and pains.

How to encourage Bible reading in your church

BRF Ministries has been helping individuals connect with the Bible for over 100 years. We want to support churches as they seek to encourage church members into regular Bible reading.

Order a Bible reading resources pack

This pack is designed to give your church the tools to publicise our Bible reading notes. It includes:

- Sample Bible reading notes for your congregation to try.
- Publicity resources, including a poster.
- A church magazine feature about Bible reading notes.

The pack is free, but we welcome a £5 donation to cover the cost of postage. If you require a pack to be sent outside the UK or require a specific number of sample Bible reading notes, please contact us for postage costs. For more information about what the current pack contains, go to **brfonline.org.uk/pages/bible-reading-resources-pack**.

How to order and find out more

- Email **enquiries@brf.org.uk**
- Phone us on +44 (0)1865 319700 Mon–Fri 9.30–17.00.
- Write to us at BRF Ministries, 15 The Chambers, Vineyard, Abingdon OX14 3FE.

Keep informed about our latest initiatives

We are continuing to develop resources to help churches encourage people into regular Bible reading, wherever they are on their journey. Join our email list at **brfonline.org.uk/signup** to stay informed about the latest initiatives that your church could benefit from.

Subscriptions

The Upper Room is published in January, May and September.

Individual subscriptions

The subscription rate for orders for 4 or fewer copies includes postage and packing:

The Upper Room annual individual subscription £25.20

Group subscriptions

Orders for 5 copies or more, sent to ONE address, are post free:
The Upper Room annual group subscription £24.75

Please do not send payment with order for a group subscription.
We will send an invoice with your first order.

Please note that the annual billing period for group subscriptions runs from 1 May to 30 April.

Copies of the notes may also be obtained from Christian bookshops.

Single copies of *The Upper Room* cost £5.99.

Prices valid until 30 April 2027.

Giant print version

The Upper Room is available in giant print for the visually impaired, from:

Torch Trust for the Blind
Torch House
Torch Way
Northampton Road
Market Harborough
LE16 9HL

Tel: +44 (0)1858 438260
torchtrust.org

THE UPPER ROOM: INDIVIDUAL/GIFT SUBSCRIPTION FORM

All our Bible reading notes can be ordered online by visiting brfonline.org.uk/subscriptions

☐ I would like to take out a subscription myself (complete your name and address details once)

☐ I would like to give a gift subscription (please provide both names and addresses)

Title .... First name/initials .... Surname ....

Address ....

.... Postcode ....

Telephone .... Email ....

Gift subscription name ....

Gift subscription address ....

.... Postcode ....

Gift message (20 words max. or include your own gift card):

....

....

Please send *The Upper Room* beginning with the May 2026 / September 2026 / January 2027 issue (*delete as appropriate*):

Annual individual subscription ☐ £25.20

Optional donation* to support the work of BRF Ministries £ ....

Total enclosed £ .... (cheques should be made payable to 'BRF')

*Please complete and return the Gift Aid declaration on page 159 to make your donation even more valuable to us.

Method of payment

Please charge my MasterCard / Visa with £ ....

Card no. ☐☐☐☐ ☐☐☐☐ ☐☐☐☐ ☐☐☐☐

Expires end M M Y Y

THE UPPER ROOM: GROUP SUBSCRIPTION FORM

All our Bible reading notes can be ordered online by visiting brfonline.org.uk/subscriptions

❑ Please send me .... copies of *The Upper Room* May 2026 / September 2026 / January 2027 issue (*delete as appropriate*)

Title .... First name/initials .... Surname ....

Address ....

.... Postcode ....

Telephone .... Email ....

Please do not send payment with this order. We will send an invoice with your first order.

Christian bookshops: All good Christian bookshops stock our resources. For your nearest stockist, please contact us.

Telephone: The BRF office is open Mon–Fri 9.30–17.00. To place your order, telephone +44 (0)1865 319700.

Online: brfonline.org.uk/group-subscriptions

❑ Please send me a Bible reading resources pack to encourage Bible reading in my church

Please return this form with the appropriate payment to:
BRF Ministries, 15 The Chambers, Vineyard, Abingdon OX14 3FE

For terms and cancellation information, please visit **brfonline.org.uk/terms**.

Bible Reading Fellowship is a charity (233280) and company limited by guarantee (301324), registered in England and Wales

To order

Online: **brfonline.org.uk**
Telephone: +44 (0)1865 319700 Mon–Fri 9.30–17.00

Delivery times within the UK are normally 15 working days. Prices are correct at the time of going to press but may change without prior notice.

BRF

Title	Price	Qty	Total
To Hell's Mouth and Back	£9.99		
Growing in Prayer	£9.99		

POSTAGE AND PACKING CHARGES			
Order value	**UK**	**Europe**	**Rest of world**
Under £7.00	£2.00	Available on request	Available on request
£7.00–£29.99	£3.00		
£30.00 and over	FREE		

Total value of books	
Postage and packing	
Donation*	
Total for this order	

* Please complete the Gift Aid declaration below

Please complete in BLOCK CAPITALS

Title .... First name/initials .... Surname ....

Address ....

.... Postcode ....

Acc. No. .... Telephone ....

Email ....

BRF Ministries Gift Aid Declaration

giftaid it

In order to Gift Aid your donation, you must tick the box below.

☐ I want to Gift Aid my donation and any donation I make in the future or have made in the past four years to BRF Ministries.

I am a UK taxpayer and understand that if I pay less Income Tax and/or Capital Gains Tax in the current tax year than the amount of Gift Aid claimed on all my donations, it is my responsibility to pay any difference.

Please notify BRF Ministries if you want to cancel this declaration, change your name or home address, or no longer pay sufficient tax on your income and/or capital gains.

Method of payment

☐ Cheque (made payable to BRF) ☐ MasterCard / Visa

Card no. ☐☐☐☐ ☐☐☐☐ ☐☐☐☐ ☐☐☐☐

Expires end M M Y Y

Please return this form to:

BRF Ministries, 15 The Chambers, Vineyard, Abingdon OX14 3FE | **enquiries@brf.org.uk**

For terms and cancellation information, please visit **brfonline.org.uk/terms**.